IMAGES
of America

IRISH ARIZONA

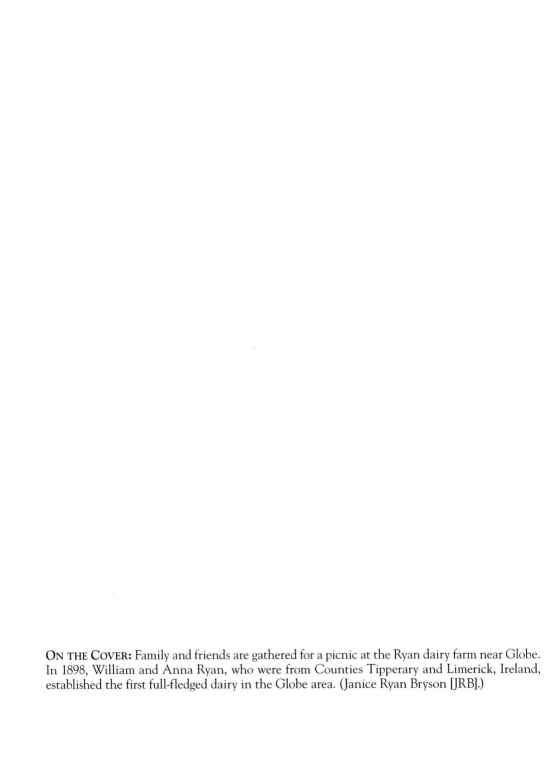

ON THE COVER: Family and friends are gathered for a picnic at the Ryan dairy farm near Globe. In 1898, William and Anna Ryan, who were from Counties Tipperary and Limerick, Ireland, established the first full-fledged dairy in the Globe area. (Janice Ryan Bryson [JRB].)

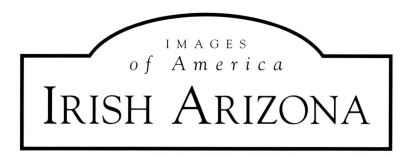

IMAGES of America
IRISH ARIZONA

Janice Ryan Bryson and
Kathleen Shappee Wood

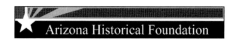

Copyright © 2008 by Janice Ryan Bryson and Kathleen Shappee Wood
ISBN 978-0-7385-5647-5

Published by Arcadia Publishing
Charleston SC, Chicago IL, Portsmouth NH, San Francisco CA

Printed in the United States of America

Library of Congress Catalog Card Number: 2008924289

For all general information contact Arcadia Publishing at:
Telephone 843-853-2070
Fax 843-853-0044
E-mail sales@arcadiapublishing.com
For customer service and orders:
Toll-Free 1-888-313-2665

Visit us on the Internet at www.arcadiapublishing.com

This book is dedicated to those of Irish origin and ancestry who helped create the state of Arizona from the raw frontier and to the memory of Kathy Shappee Wood

CONTENTS

Acknowledgments		6
Foreword		7
Introduction		8
1.	Early Days in the Arizona Territory	11
2.	Land of Opportunity	23
3.	The Long Arm of the Law	81
4.	Religion, Education, and Healing	105
5.	Irish Arizona Today	119
Bibliography		127

ACKNOWLEDGMENTS

Creating a book that covers the whole state of Arizona is no small task. It could not have been completed without the generous support of many individuals. Thanks to the historical societies of Gila County, Pinal County, and Mohave County, as well as the historical societies of Sedona, Glendale, Jerome (Ronne Roope, archivist), Prescott's Sharlot Hall Museum, and the Prescott Public Library. The Arizona Historical Society in Tucson was a valuable source, as was the Bisbee Mining and Historical Museum. We also obtained photographs and made use of references from the Arizona Room of the Phoenix Public Library, Arizona State Capital Library Archives, and Arizona State University's Hayden Library. The Arizona Historical Foundation is to be commended for sharing their photographs and Arizona history records with the authors of Arcadia books. Thanks also to the Dougherty Foundation, Loyola Marymount University, Riordan Mansion State Historic Park, Marshall Trimble, and Sr. Madonna Marie Bolton of St. Joseph's Hospital for their contributions to our book. The *Desert Shamrock* newspaper generously provided pictures of the Irish in Arizona today, as did the Irish in Tucson. Our special thanks go to Pat Bonn for all her assistance and support and to Len Wood for his encouragement. Thanks to our friends and families, who shared their treasured photographs and stories of the Irish in Arizona. The descendants of the Irish families in our book have always been proud of their families' history in Arizona and generous to a fault in sharing it. Thanks to Kelly, Ryan, Karimy, Colten, Austin, Ximena, and Walter for having patience with a mother/grandmother who hauled them all over Arizona to every historical site imaginable. Thanks also to our Arcadia editor, Jared Jackson.

Go raibh míle maith agaibh! (Thanks a million!)

Foreword

There's an old saying about "the luck of the Irish," referring to a person who struck it rich in the mining camps of the West. For a few Irish immigrants that was true. Others made it through pure hard work and honest determination. Nellie Cashman immigrated to America from County Cork and headed west to seek her fortune. She opened boardinghouses and restaurants all over the West. Despite her business success, she's best known as the "Miner's Angel" for her kindness and generosity.

Nathan Oakes Murphy, the likely descendant of Ulster Irish, was twice appointed territorial governor and was a territorial delegate to Congress. His brother Frank was one of the territory's greatest entrepreneurs, opening mines and building railroads such as the line from Ash Fork to Phoenix linking the capital city to the transcontinental mainline. Another Murphy, William J., built the Arizona canal leading to the founding of Scottsdale and communities in the West Valley. His parents were from County Antrim, Northern Ireland.

William "Buckey" O'Neill, the son of Irish-born parents, arrived in Phoenix in 1879 and worked as a reporter before heading to Tombstone during the days of "helldorado." Moving to Prescott, he was elected sheriff of Yavapai County. Buckey was one of Arizona's most flamboyant figures capturing outlaws and was a member of Teddy Roosevelt's famous Rough Riders in the Spanish-American War.

These well-known Arizona figures are just the tip of the iceberg for all the unsung Irish who worked as cowboys, built the railroads, worked in the mines, owned businesses, became professionals, and worked the land. Through hard work, Irish pride, and perseverance, they contributed to the building of a state and left an indelible mark on the history of Arizona.

The Irish Arizona Project is continuing research to collect the stories of those of Irish birth and ancestry who came to Arizona and applied their scrappy persistence to a land that sorely needed their drive for survival.

—Marshall Trimble
Official Arizona State Historian

INTRODUCTION

Janice Ryan Bryson and Kathleen Wood converged from very different orientations in their search for pioneers of Irish birth and ancestry in Territorial Arizona. Their research culminates in *Irish Arizona*. This book identifies a few famous and many unheralded Irish pioneers who made their mark as ranchers, merchants, miners, lawmen, explorers, soldiers, and healers in an untamed wilderness.

Janice, honored as a 2008 Arizona Culture Keeper, has spent several years researching her Irish ancestors, who came to Arizona in the early 1880s, by gathering photographs and interviewing family members. This allowed her to collect not only genealogical data but also the stories that bring these resolute people to life.

While she was studying the Irish language, Kathy, a bagpiper, learned of an obscure but significant connection between Ireland and Arizona. Often called Gaelic, the Irish language had become almost extinct by the late 1800s. Three men, including the Irish priest Eugene O'Growney, founded the Gaelic League with the objective of bringing the Irish language back into common use; chapters of the league spread throughout Ireland and the world. O'Growney came to Arizona in 1896 in hopes of curing his tuberculosis. He spent much of his time in the care of the Irish-born Sisters of Mercy, founders of St. Joseph's Hospital in Phoenix. Among his friends was Michael Riordan of Flagstaff, a proud son of Irish immigrants.

In Colonial times, the Irish population in America was second only to that of the English. The majority of these early Irish immigrants were Scotch-Irish Protestants who left Northern Ireland due to religious conflicts and dire economic conditions. Irish Catholics also came in smaller numbers during this period. Most were educated and skilled workers settling in Pennsylvania, Virginia, and the Carolinas.

Irish immigration to America began to increase in 1816. Many of those arrivals built the Erie Canal and laid steel and timber for railroad tracks. One journalist commented, "There are several kinds of power working for the republic—water-power, steam-power, and Irish-power, the last works hardest of all."

In the 1840s, *An Gorta Mór* ("the great hunger" in Gaelic), known as the Irish Potato Famine, launched an unprecedented exodus to America and elsewhere. Most of these immigrants settled close to the port cities where they disembarked, having little money for traveling or purchasing land, settling in already-established Irish communities.

The prospect of striking it rich in California prompted immigrants and citizens alike to leave their homes and try their luck during the 1849 Gold Rush. The discovery of gold and silver elsewhere in the West tested the persistence and endurance of those who came after the Civil War to face the region's Native Americans, harsh terrain, and extreme climates. When the earth did not yield a fortune, many immigrants discovered they could find success by feeding and supplying the miners and military posts gaining a toehold in a hostile land.

As Janice and Kathy compared notes, they realized the Irish in Arizona didn't behave the way they did in cities where Irish immigrants had historically concentrated. The Irish didn't come to

Arizona in the large numbers they did elsewhere, and the sheer effort to survive did not afford them the opportunity and leisure to create the fraternal and benevolent organizations typical of other large Irish American populations. Often they had made many stops along the way, through common points of Irish immigration like New York City and San Francisco, and many had been to other places around the world—Africa, South America, Australia—following the promise of fortune.

In 2006, Janice and Kathy started the nonprofit Irish Arizona Project, dedicated to collecting the stories of those of Irish birth and ancestry who came to Arizona in territorial times and in the early years of the young state. The story of the Irish in Arizona bears elements of immigration and nativism and religious and ethnic prejudice that are still relevant. It also examines a unique population not typically associated with the American southwest, shedding light on social and family dynamics in a unique way.

As Celtic music, culture, and art grow in popularity in Arizona and elsewhere in the United States, *Irish Arizona* fills a niche by collecting and preserving the stories and images of a previously overlooked population of Irish pioneers who survived and thrived in the American southwest.

One

EARLY DAYS IN THE ARIZONA TERRITORY

Imagine what life was like for the first explorers, pathfinders, and settlers in Arizona. Forget comfort, forget roads and road maps, forget safety and security. These people came to the southwest based on hearsay and legend, their dreams fleshing out the image of what life would be like for them in this place.

Extremes of climate and terrain made it difficult enough to get to what is now Arizona, let alone find ways to survive. Those who persisted found evidence of ancient native settlements, including ruins of large adobe dwellings and miles of irrigation canals; they also found a range of welcomes from natives who still lived there, some peaceful and some engaging with these white invaders in a mutual battle of domination and extermination.

Conventional American history often ignores national origin when historians consider the lives and actions of historical figures. When this detail is taken into account, it is possible to get a different impression and a bigger picture of events and the people who brought them about. In the case of Hugo O'Conor, for example, history generally commemorates him as simply the representative of the government of Spain who established the presidio of Tucson. If we know he was born in Ireland and was, in fact, one of the legendary Wild Geese, men exiled from Ireland into service for Catholic monarchs abroad due to the ethnic and religious bigotry of English domination at home, we have a historical connection with much greater impact and scope.

Hugo O'Conor was born in Dublin, Ireland, in 1734 to a noble Irish Catholic family. He fled to Spain as one of Ireland's Wild Geese to join the Spanish army in opposition to the English. After serving in Cuba as a member of Spain's Hibernian Regiment, O'Conor went to what is now Texas to organize Spanish troops against the Comanches and Apaches. He served the Spanish in Arizona as well; this statue of Hugo O'Conor stands in Tucson. (JRB.)

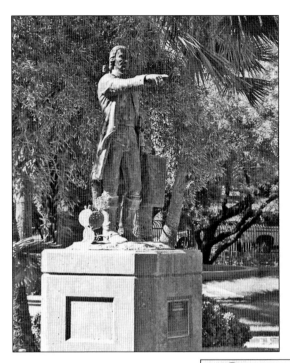

In August 1775, O'Conor signed a document on behalf of the king of Spain establishing the presidio of Tucson. He became known as El Capitán Colorado, the red captain. (Arizona Historical Society.)

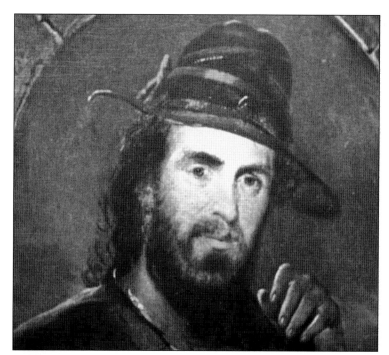

Joseph Reddeford Walker, a mountain man of Scotch-Irish descent, was born in Tennessee in 1798. He is believed to have first visited Arizona about 1837–1838. Following the demise of the Rocky Mountain fur operations, he trapped, traded, and served as a guide throughout the West. Walker organized the Walker Party in 1861, which opened up central Arizona through their exploration. (Marshall Trimble.)

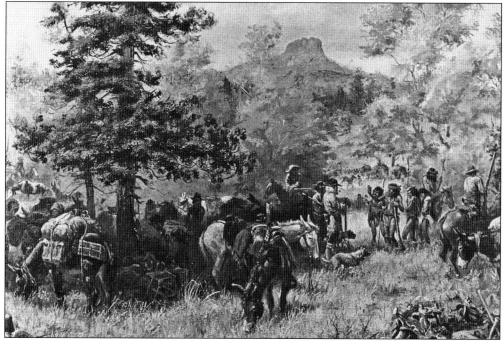

Walker's group traveled to Southern Arizona and came up the Hassayampa River to Granite Creek close to the present site of Prescott. Gold was soon discovered in Lynx Creek. The "Walker diggings" developed quickly and lead to the settlement that incorporated the first major capital of the Arizona Territory. *The Walker Party* shows Captain Walker at the site where gold was discovered. Thumb Butte can be seen in the background. (Painting by George Phippen, 1964; City of Prescott Public Library.)

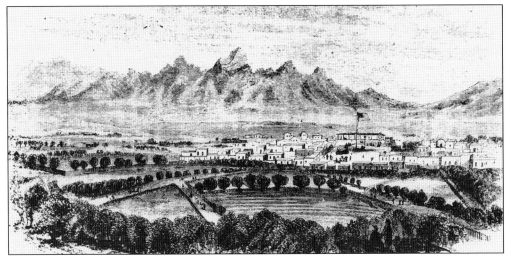

Mexican troops had to evacuate Tucson after the U.S. government paid $10 million to Mexico in 1854 for the Gadsden Purchase. Fourteen Americans were in Tucson in February 1855, including two Irishmen, Paddy Burke and William Finley. Over the objections of the Mexican commander, the Americans took down the Mexican flag during the troop evacuation and raised the American flag. This sketch of Tucson was drawn from an 1862 wartime photograph. (Sketch by Palatine Robinson; Arizona Historical Society/Tucson #59398.)

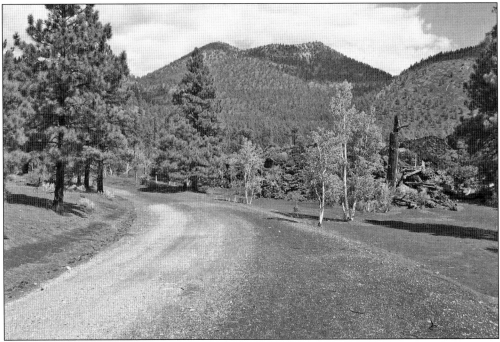

Daniel O'Leary was born around 1843 in Ireland. He served as guide, interpreter, and mountain man for military and other endeavors. An 1867 letter published in Prescott's *Daily Arizona Miner* discusses the U.S. Army's battles against the Hualapai Indians: "Our worthy townsmen, Geo Spear and Dan O'Leary go as guides; better and more thorough mountaineers than Kit Carson ever was or will be." O'Leary Peak in Coconino County is named for him. (Scott Surgent and Beth Cousland.)

John Ward was born in Ireland in 1806. Described as "a somber colored son of Erin," Ward established a ranch in the Sonoita Valley. Seven farms were located in the valley, one belonging to fellow Irishman Felix Grundy Ake. Tragedy struck when Ward's stepson, Felix Telles, was kidnapped by Apaches. The Apaches created a great financial hardship for Ward when they drove off all of his cattle in 1867. The ruins of John Ward's ranch are shown here in 1913. (Arizona Historical Society/Tucson #55511.)

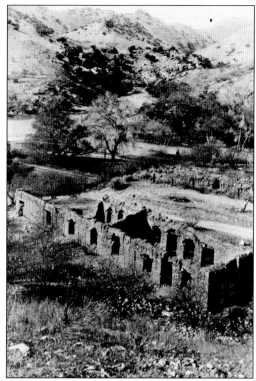

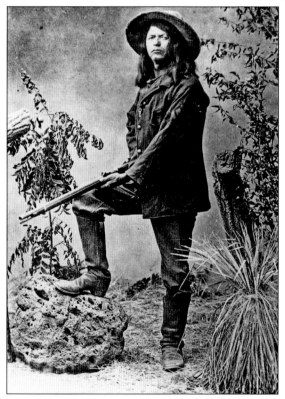

John Ward's stepson, 13-year-old Felix Telles, was captured by Apaches during a raid on the Ward Ranch in 1861. Felix, of Mexican descent, was often mistaken as half-Irish. He was given the name Mickey Free by the U.S. Army when he enlisted as an Indian scout. In 1886, Mickey travelled as interpreter with the Apache delegation to Washington, D.C., to meet President Cleveland. A newspaper prematurely reported his death in 1913, noting, "He had a face as Irish as his name, a heart as large as the Irish superstition and wit and was loved by the Indian and white men on the Reservation." (Arizona Historical Society/Tucson, Gatewood Collection #19724.)

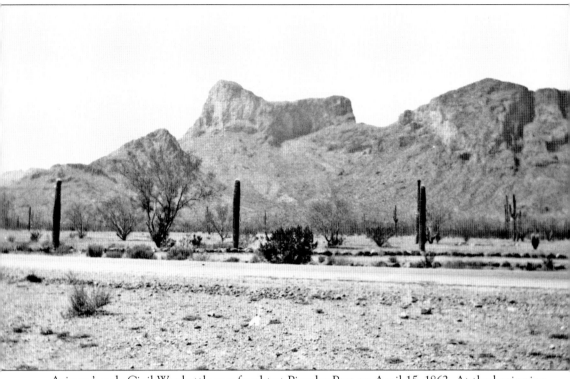

Arizona's only Civil War battle was fought at Picacho Pass on April 15, 1862. At the beginning of the Civil War, the U.S. government began calling back the majority of the army stationed in the West. New Mexico Territory was declared for the Confederacy. Troops were stationed in Tucson awaiting the arrival of the Union army's California Column. Pima Indians, loyal to the federal government, had advised Capt. William Calloway that 10 Confederates had a picket guard at Picacho Pass. Calloway planned to have Lt. James Barrett, a County Mayo native, approach Picacho from the east and Lt. Ephraim Baldwin approach from the west to cut off the picket's line of retreat and march to Tucson to surprise the Confederate garrison. Lieutenant Barrett arrived well in advance of the other troops and, against advice, led a charge, his troops firing as they advanced. Three Confederates were captured. However, Lieutenant Barrett was fatally wounded while detaining them. The remaining pickets made their way to their horses and raced to Tucson to advise their superiors of the Union army's presence. (Arizona State University, Hayden Library, Hayden Collection #CP FIB3.1.)

James Lee was born in Londonderry, Ireland, in 1833. Lee arrived in Tucson in 1857 with the Overland Mail Company. After time in Mexico, Lee and William Scott developed a water power mill south of Tucson known as Jimmie Lee. Water rights obtained on the Santa Cruz River ran the mill and irrigated surrounding farms. Union troops took over the Jimmie Lee during the Civil War. Eagle Mill, a new steam mill, was constructed by Lee in 1870. (Arizona Historical Society/Tucson #14300.)

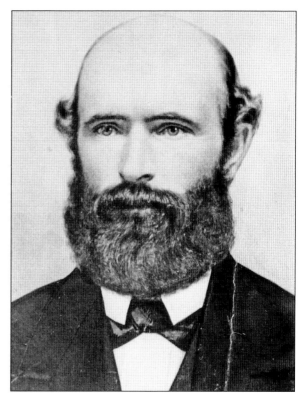

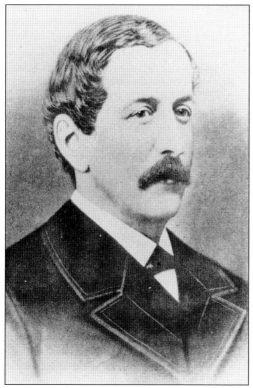

Richard Cunningham McCormick, whose ancestors hailed from Ulster, Ireland, was born in New York. In 1863, he was appointed secretary of the Arizona Territory by President Lincoln. McCormick is credited with designing the first state seal. He launched two newspapers, the *Arizona Miner* and Tucson's *Arizona Citizen*. Pres. Andrew Johnson nominated McCormick as governor of the Arizona Territory in 1866. (Arizona Historical Society/Tucson #44977.)

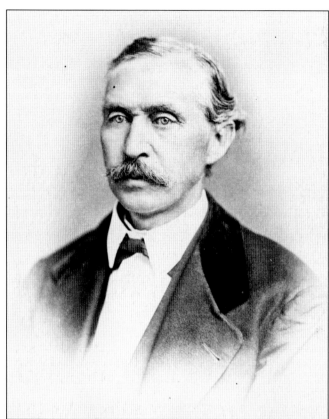

George Martin was born in 1832 in County Galway. He was educated in Dublin and apprenticed at age 10 to a doctor. Immediately upon arrival in New York City, Martin enlisted in the U.S. Army. Serving as quartermaster and hospital steward, he was stationed at Fort Yuma on the Colorado River. Discharged in 1856, Martin managed the Sutler store and opened a store in Gila City. During the Civil War, Martin partnered with King Woolsey on a ranch on the Gila River. (Arizona Historical Society/Tucson #48718.)

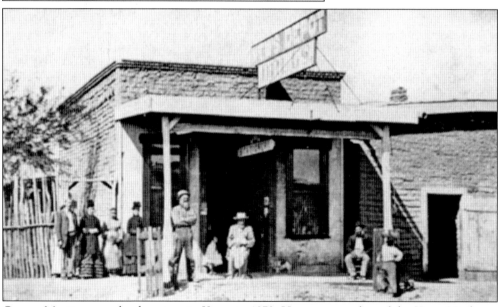

George Martin opened a drugstore in Yuma in 1872. He was a member of the Yuma Vigilance Committee and served terms as the City of Yuma treasurer and councilman. Martin also served as Yuma County supervisor and treasurer. Individuals pictured at the store are not identified. (A. Martin Ronstadt.)

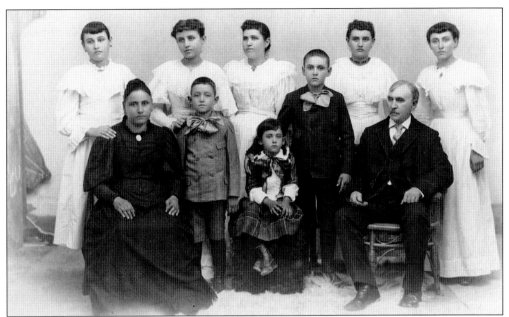

George Martin married Delfina Redondo, daughter of Sonoran land owner Esteven Redondo, in 1872. The family moved to Tucson in 1884. Pictured from left to right are (first row) Delphina (Redondo) Martin, Andrew, Louis, George Jr., and George Sr.; (second row) Stephena (Martin) Kaal, Matilda (Martin) Ronstadt, Mary Martin, Delphina (Martin) Duffy, and Agnes (Martin) Clark. (Arizona Historical Society/Tucson #16556.)

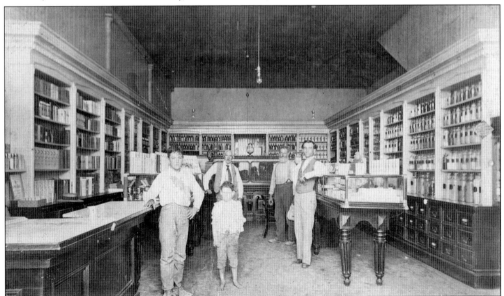

Martin opened the Dr. Martin Drug stores in Tucson. The title of doctor was acquired from his training in Ireland and the military. Eight Martin Drug stores were opened in Tucson, making them the city's first chain store. Dr. Martin installed Arizona's first soda fountain in 1885. The drugstore at 28 West Congress Street is shown in this 1898 picture. Pictured from left to right are George Martin Jr., George Martin Sr., Andrew Martin, ? Hughes, and Sylvester Percell. (Arizona Historical Society/Tucson #45169.)

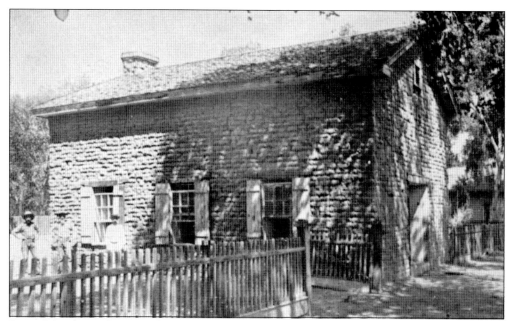

James Monihan, the son of Irish parents, was a real estate agent in early Phoenix. In the summer of 1871, he and his partner, Capt. William Hancock, built the first designated Maricopa County Courthouse on First Avenue, south of Washington Street. The construction cost of the adobe building, later used as Phoenix's first public school, amounted to $900. (Arizona Historical Foundation.)

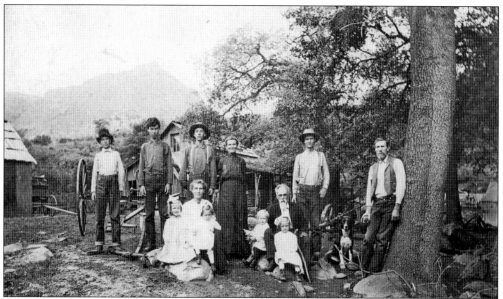

John James Thompson was the first Anglo settler to permanently reside in Oak Creek Canyon. Born in Londonderry, Thompson left Ireland at age 14. He was able to talk his way onto a ship leaving Liverpool, convincing a young man to purchase his ticket as his younger brother. Thompson traveled widely in America before arriving in the Arizona Territory. He came across Indian Gardens in 1876 after the Apaches had left the area. Thompson and his wife, Margaret, are pictured in Oak Creek Canyon with their children and grandchildren. (Sedona Historical Society.)

James Reilly came to New York from County Cavan with his mother in 1848. After serving in the army, Reilly engaged in freighting in America and Mexico. He was a businessman in Yuma, Yavapai, and Maricopa Counties. Reilly was admitted to the Arizona Bar, and in 1880, he headed for Tombstone to open a law office. Appointed justice of the peace, he also represented Cochise County in the 17th Territorial Legislature. In this edited picture of the Cochise County Bar in 1883, Reilly is shown between Col. William Herring (left) and Thomas Mitchell. (Arizona Historical Foundation.)

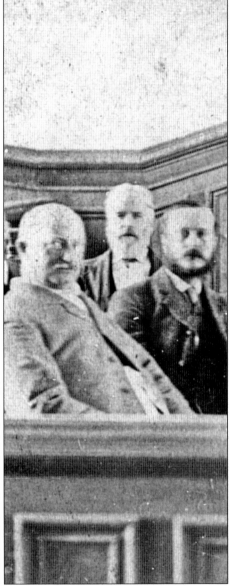

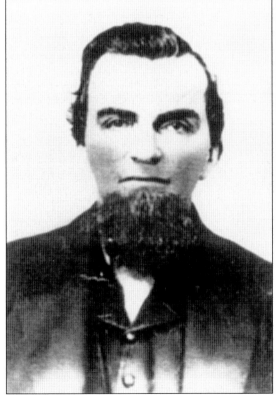

Irishman Christopher Baine settled in Yuma in the 1870s. He was the designer and maker of Baine covered wagons. The 1880 census shows Baine; wife, Jesus Dominquez; and six children living in Phoenix. (Frank Barrios.)

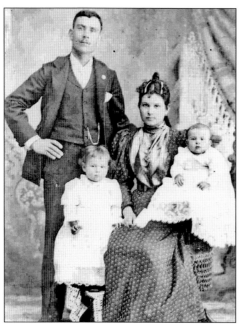

Christopher Baine's daughter Juanita married José Monteverde Iberri. He was a wealthy businessman who owned Phoenix stores, large parcels of land in South Phoenix, and a cattle operation east of Mesa. The couple had 19 children. (Frank Barrios.)

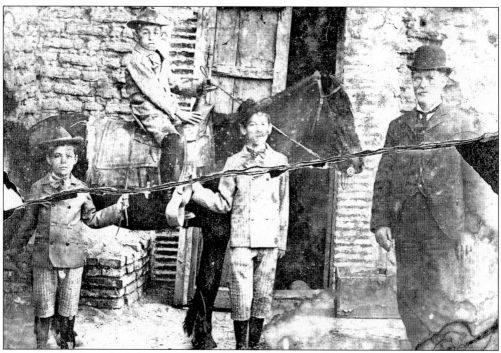

Louis "Luis" Killeen (right) was born in Ireland in the 1850s. He was probably a very young man when he and his two brothers came to America. He obtained American citizenship and went to Mexico, where he became a successful entrepreneur, building a hotel and owning agricultural and mining interests. He married Antonina Hernandez in Ures, Sonora, in 1887. Shown here from left to right are their three sons: Art, Armand, and Louis. The Killeens fled to Phoenix as refugees during the Mexican Revolution. Louis Killeen started the Rex Theatre around 1910, which catered to the Mexican community with Spanish language entertainment. (Frank Barrios.)

Two

LAND OF OPPORTUNITY

The hardy individuals who dared to settle in the Arizona Territory were a special breed of men and women. Relative comforts were often given up in other places to begin a new life on the frontier. Arizona quickly became known for a potential wealth in minerals. As mining communities began to be established all over Arizona, so did supporting elements such as roads, forts, commerce, ranching, and agriculture. Growing up in Arizona, school children learned the five Cs that supported the economy of the state—copper, cattle, climate, citrus, and cotton.

Miners, smelter workers, gamblers, freighters, saloon and storekeepers, teachers, wives, and children arrived in the territory searching for a better life. Despite great risk and difficulties, the Irish had a better chance of improving their lot in life in the wild land of Apacheria than in the Ireland of the late 1800s with the political unrest existing at that time.

The Irish showed rugged individualism and left behind a wonderful legacy and a rich history of Arizona with their stories.

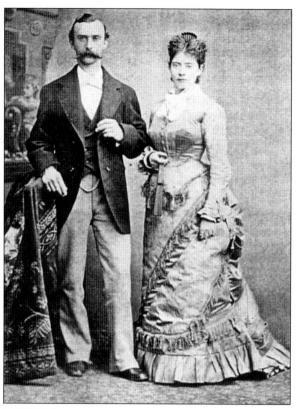

John Holohan came from Kilkee, Ireland, to Chicago, later settling San Francisco. Annie Ryan arrived in Wisconsin from County Tipperary, also making her way to San Francisco. The couple met in that city, where John had a saloon. Moving to the Arizona Territory in 1879, John worked at the McMorris mines in Richmond Basin. (JRB.)

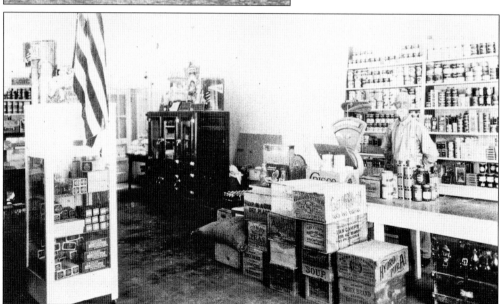

Within a short time of arrival, John Holohan rented a store in Globe and opened a saloon. He sold that enterprise, using the money to buy cattle to stock a ranch near McMillan. The family lived at the ranch at times and in Globe. John also had investments in mining. He began buying property in Phoenix, opening a grocery store and rental apartments. One property, at Central Avenue and Fillmore Street, was sold to the U.S. post office. (JRB.)

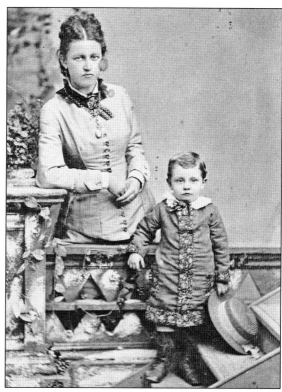

Julia Murphy had her picture taken in San Francisco with little Johnny Holohan, son of her friends John and Annie Holohan, shortly before the Holohans moved to Arizona. Three sons and three daughters were born to the couple in Arizona. Three sons and three daughters were born in Arizona. Childhood diseases took a heavy toll in the territory each year. Johnny's three younger brothers died of diphtheria in 1886 within two days of each other. Johnny himself was shot and killed at 16 during a roundup near Globe. The inquest ruled the shooting an accident, a verdict never accepted by the family. (JRB.)

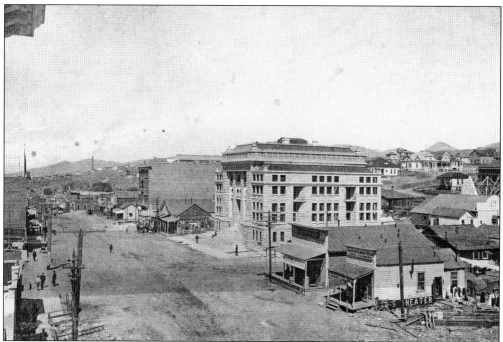

Globe was founded in 1876 as a part of Pinal County. In early 1881, the rich mineral district was separated from Pinal County, and Globe was named as county seat of the newly created Gila County. (JRB.)

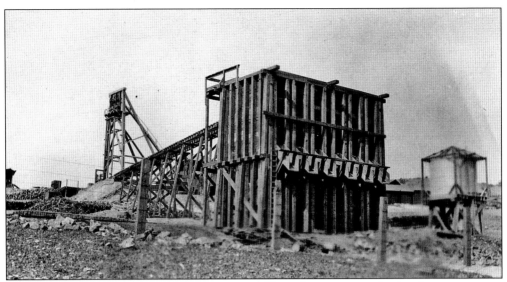

The discovery of copper in the Twin Buttes region of Pima County is accredited to three prospectors known as "The Three Nations"—John G. Baxter from Wisconsin, Michael Irish from Ireland, and John Ellis from Scotland. After struggling for years, they convinced prominent investors to take over the property in 1903. Twin Buttes Mining and Smelting developed and operated the Senator, Morgan, Copper Glance, Copper Queen, and Copper King Mines. (Arizona Historical Foundation, McClintock Collection.)

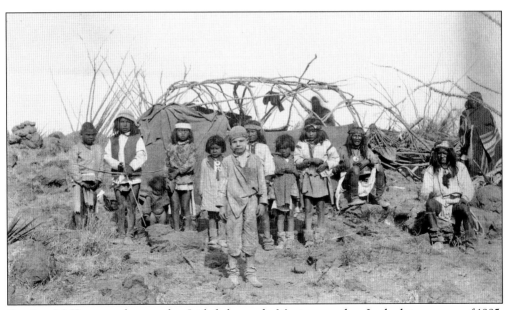

Santiago McKinn was the son of an Irish father and a Mexican mother. In the late summer of 1885, Geronimo attacked the family's small ranch near Deming, New Mexico. Santiago and his brother were there herding cattle. The older brother was killed, and Santiago was captured. In April 1886, Native American prisoners were brought to Fort Bowie; Santiago was among them. At the fort, he cried and refused to leave the Native Americans. Santiago was forcibly taken to the train to return home. (Arizona State Library, History and Archives Division/Phoenix #97-2656.)

William Ryan, a native of County Tipperary, arrived in New York in 1878. He spent a few months there before heading to the coalfields of Pennsylvania. William then drifted west to Missouri, Colorado, and New Mexico, arriving in Arizona on the banks of Pinal Creek in January 1881. His first job was that of a mail carrier for the McMillan Silver Mine. (JRB.)

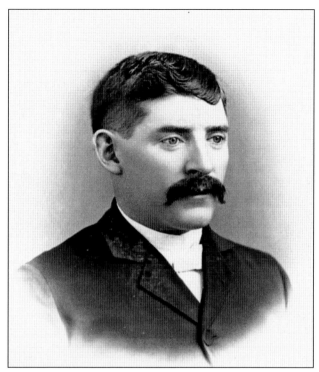

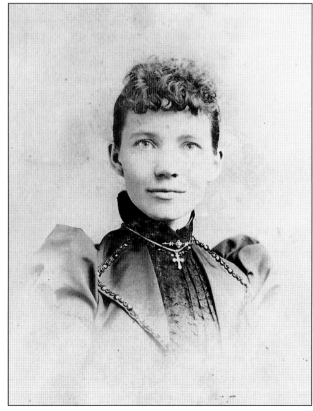

Anna Mary Moloney hailed from Cloverfield, County Limerick. Anna had been told by her uncle Denis Murphy that he would send for her if he did well in America. In 1883, she sailed to America alone at the age of 16. She disembarked in New York and traveled by train to visit relatives in San Francisco before continuing her journey by train and stagecoach to join her uncle Denis in Globe. (JRB.)

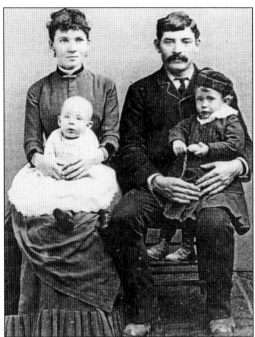

William Ryan and Anna Moloney were married in Globe in October 1884 by Fr. Eduard Gerard. The couple is pictured here around 1888 with their first two children, baby Cornelius Michael and two-year-old William Albert. (JRB.)

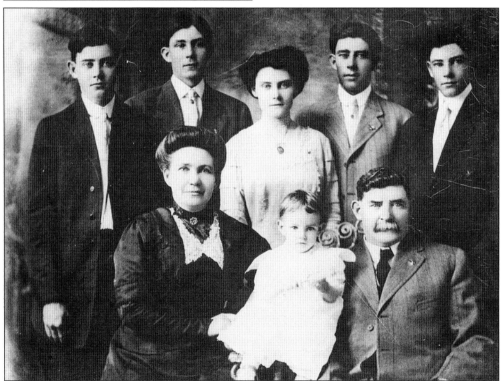

After several years in Hatchita, New Mexico, and Chicago for less than a year, the William Ryan family returned to Globe. They believed their future lay in the Arizona Territory. Pictured from left to right are (first row) Anna, Alice, and William; (second row) Edward Emmet, Cornelius Michael, Mary (May), William Albert, and Joseph Bernard. (JRB.)

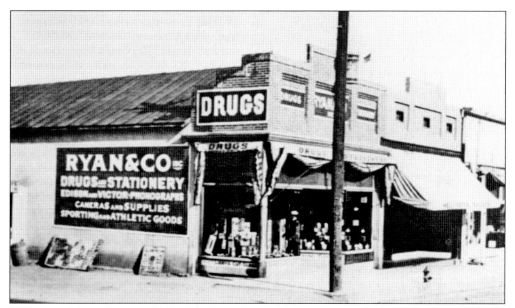

William and Anna Ryan established the Ryan Company Store in 1904, dealing in books, periodicals, and stationery. William continued to pursue his mining and livestock interests, with Anna assuming much of the responsibility of the store. In 1907, Anna's brother, John Moloney, joined the firm. (JRB.)

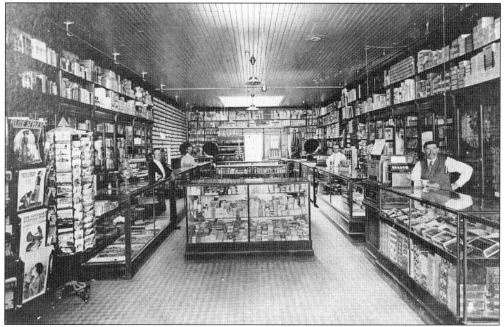

Ryan and Company continued to expand, adding a line of sporting goods, phonographs and records, guns, and ammunition. Son Joseph joined the firm as a pharmacist and expanded the stores from Gila County to Phoenix. Larry Evans was a partner for a while, and the Ryan Company became Ryan-Evans. William Ryan is pictured on the right front, and John Moloney is behind him in this 1908 photograph from Globe. The employees are unidentified. In the mid-1960s, Ryan-Evans's chain of 35 Arizona stores was sold to Revco. (JRB.)

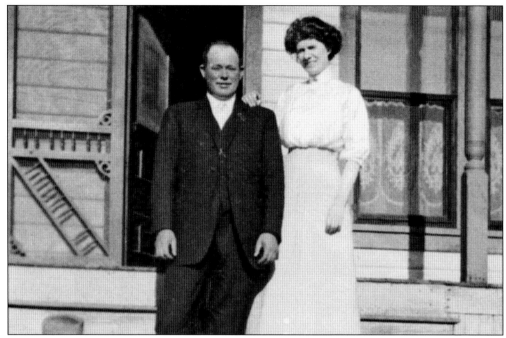

Julia Ryan arrived in Globe from County Tipperary, as did her brother Joseph "Smokey Joe" Ryan. He was given his nickname for his baseball pitching skills. Julia is pictured in 1912 with her fiancé, Robert Mackey, on the day of their wedding. The ceremony was held at the home of her cousin Margaret Ryan Murphy in Globe. The couple lived in Bisbee, where Mackey was employed as a mining engineer. (JRB.)

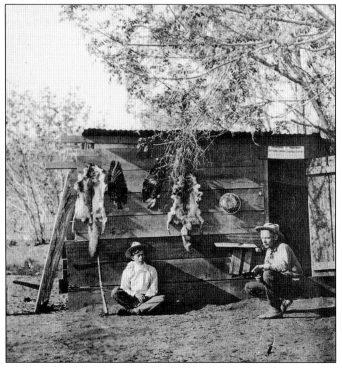

Young William Albert "Bill" Ryan (left) and Ranger Jones are pictured here at Bill's trapping camp near Globe. The son of William and Anna, Bill was typical of the children of the western pioneers. Young boys worked on family ranches and farms, trapped, and worked as laborers or at odd jobs in town to help provide a better living for their families. The mining industry was hazardous, and many men died, leaving a widow and children. Working was often a necessity for all members of the family to survive the harsh conditions in the territory. (JRB.)

Denis Murphy was born in County Limerick, growing up on his family farm in Ireland. He arrived in New York in 1880 at age 24. After a short time there, Denis traveled to San Francisco and worked in Northern California. Hearing of mining successes in the Arizona Territory, he traveled to Globe, where his first job was driving a team hauling wood to the mines. (JRB.)

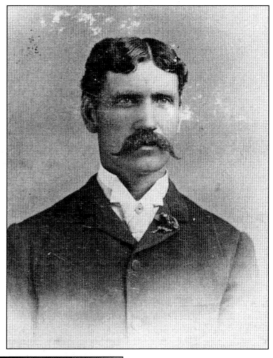

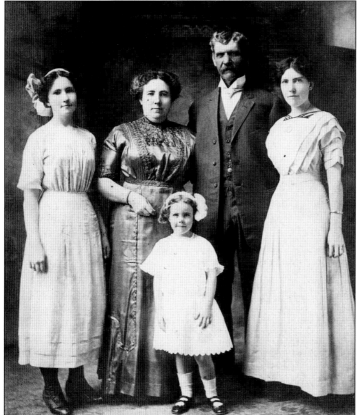

Denis traveled back to Ireland and met Margaret Ryan, cousin of the Globe Ryans. They were married on March 17, 1889, in Ireland, returned to Globe, and became the parents of three daughters. Pictured from left to right are Marguerite, Margaret, Denis, and Josephine. Daughter Muriel stands in front. In 1907, Denis was one of seven men named to form a new city government in Globe. The family moved to Los Angeles in 1912. Denis kept many of his businesses in Globe and traveled there frequently from California. (JRB.)

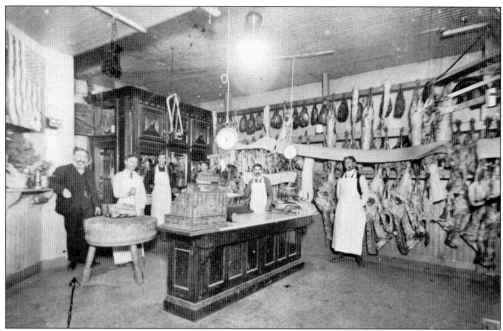

Denis Murphy is shown on the left with the employees of his meat market in Globe. He and several other local men owned butcher shops. They would slaughter their cattle outside of town, doing the work at night. The meat would be cooled in the evening, brought into town before daylight, and hung in homemade iceboxes. The shops were usually sold out by noon and remained closed until the next morning. (JRB.)

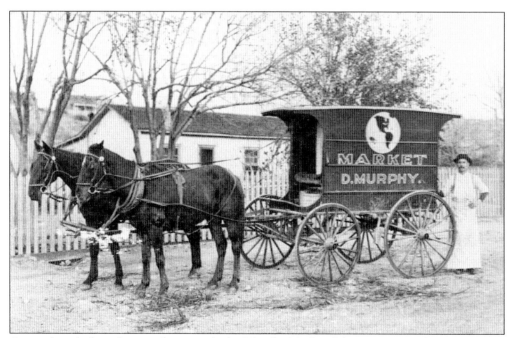

An unidentified employee is shown with the Murphy Market delivery wagon. The meat market offered delivery service to the residents of Globe. (JRB.)

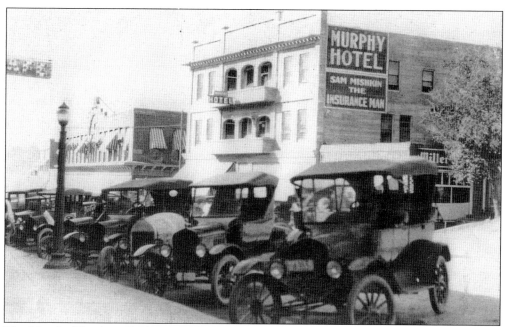

The Murphy Hotel was built in 1916 by Denis Murphy. Denis was very active in civic affairs in Globe. (JRB.)

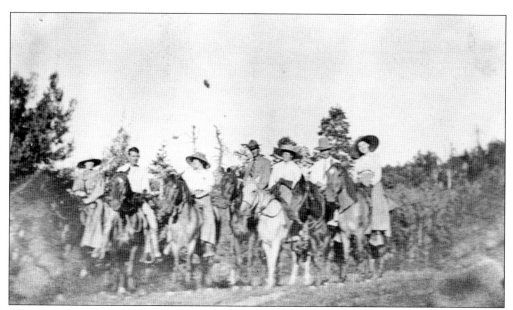

The young people in the early days of the territory depended on their own two feet or horses for transportation. Josephine Murphy and her fiancé, Michael Doran, are pictured on the left with unidentified friends at Six Shooter Canyon outside of Globe. (JRB.)

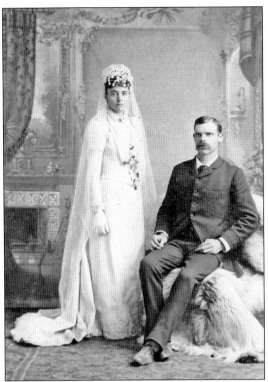

John Murphy was born in Ireland and settled in Butte, Montana. He was sent to Globe in the late 1880s to organize and build the Old Dominion Smelter, becoming its first superintendent. He married a schoolteacher, a French girl named Esther. She died in childbirth with their first child. John died a young man as the result of food poisoning. (JRB.)

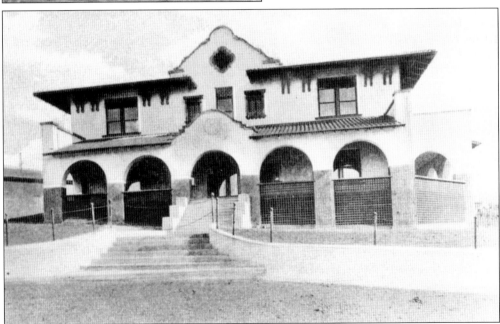

John Murphy donated a house and land in Globe to the city. The site became the home of the Old Dominion Library. The library was built by the Old Dominion Company in honor of three men who died in the Interloper Mine fire. The library burned in 1979, and Globe suffered the loss of the books, as well as history and pictures of the early years of their city. (Gila County Historical Society.)

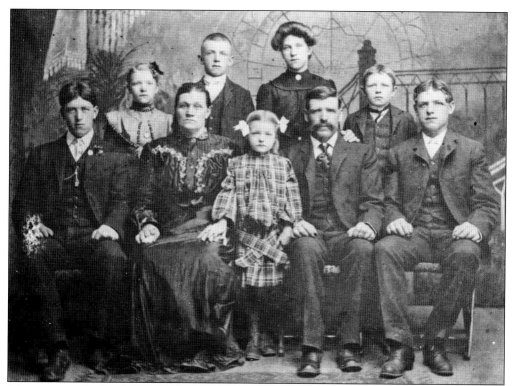

John wrote to his brother, Joseph Murphy, in Butte asking to join him in Globe. Joseph and his wife, Mary O'Leary, arrived in Globe in 1902 with their children. Joseph was instrumental in getting the workers at the Old Dominion unionized. Their son Michael served in the Arizona Legislature representing Gila County. He introduced the bill creating the highway department. Shown here from left to right (first row) are John, Mary, Nell, Joseph, and Michael; (second row) Kate, Joseph, Mayme, and Edward. (Colleen Mercer.)

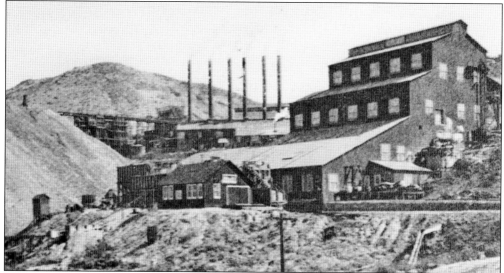

Mining in the Globe zone was overpowered by the vast operations of the Old Dominion Mine. In 1910, the company included nine claims, a smelter, and a mill site. (Gila County Historical Society.)

John J. Moloney was born in County Limerick and came to Globe to visit his sister, Anna Ryan, and uncle, Denis Murphy, on his way to Australia. He liked Arizona and decided to stay. John worked with Anna and her husband, William, in their dairy and purchased his uncle Denis's meat market. In 1907, he was secretary-treasurer of Ryan and Company. John loved to travel, returning to Ireland twice. He met his wife, Mary Kelley, in San Francisco. (JRB.)

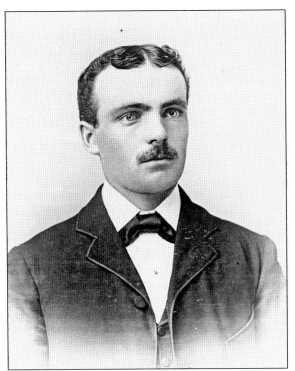

Mary Alice (May) Kelley was born in San Francisco, the daughter of Mary Mulcahy and Michael Kelley. Michael's parents were early settlers in California, and he was born in the infamous Hangtown (Placerville). May attended a secretarial school and worked for a lumber company in San Francisco, the city where she married John Moloney in 1913. The couple made their first home in Claypool. (JRB.)

Patrick Shanley was born in England, his parents having immigrated there from Ireland. After fighting for the United States in the Civil War, Patrick went west and eventually settled in McMillan, where he ran a freight company between there and Globe. He served as superintendent of the Gila County Commissioners. Patrick was a cattle rancher and also owned a butcher shop. His advertisement featured his cattle brand, the Cross S. (*Arizona Silverbelt* advertisement, 1890.)

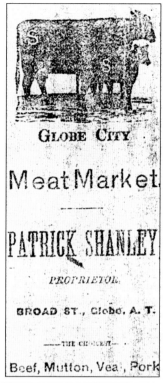

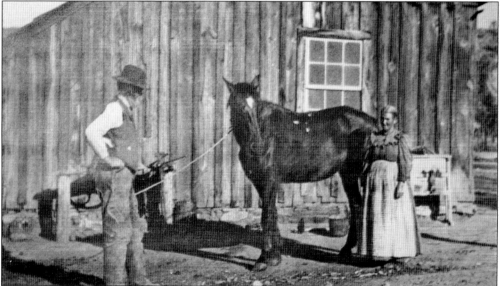

Henry Armer was one of the Irish who built the Erie Canal, working as a muleskinner. He met Lucinda Heberd in Oregon, and after time spent in Washington and California, the couple headed to Arizona. They made their home north of the Salt River at what became known as Armer Gulch. In 1903, the federal government purchased the farms along the Salt River to build Roosevelt Dam, and the couple moved to Livingston, which in turn was covered by Roosevelt Lake. After Henry's death, Lucinda grazed cattle in the Sierra Ancha District. (Gila County Historical Society.)

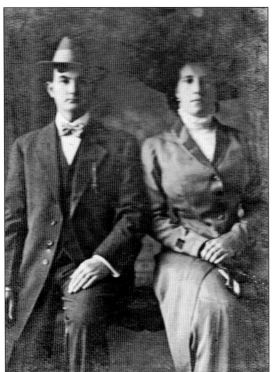

John Philip McNeil, an orphan, traveled from County Tipperary to America by himself around 1898. He married Rosella Whitmer and settled into life in Globe. Later establishing businesses in Miami, John was a great booster of the city and worked for better streets, schools, and more arteries of commerce into Miami in the form of concrete roads. (Sharon Mangum Ricart.)

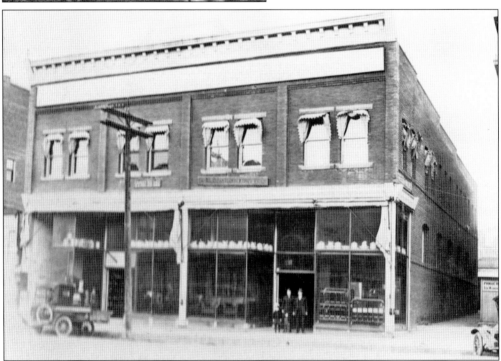

John McNeil started in the furniture business in Globe, later opening a store in Miami. He is pictured with his family in front of his Globe store, located in the Sultan Building on Broad Street. (Sharon Mangum Ricart.)

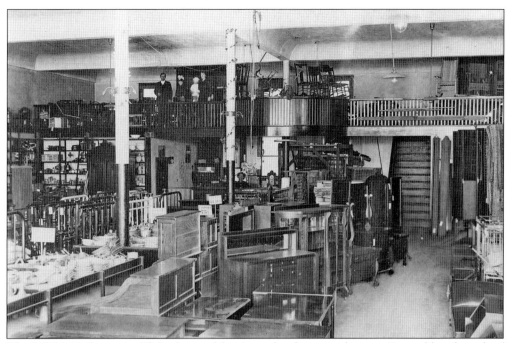

The J. P. McNeil store in Globe featured furniture, hardware, and stoves. Second-hand goods of all kinds were bought and sold, some even on a lease basis. (Sharon Mangum Ricart.)

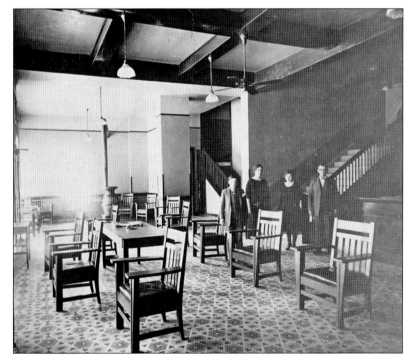

Pictured here from left to right are John Jr., Rosella, Catherine, and John Sr. in the lobby of their McNeil Hotel in Miami. The hotel was a three-story concrete building with 65 rooms, including apartments. One writer noted the hotel was beautifully furnished with modern furniture and baths. (Sharon Mangum Ricart.)

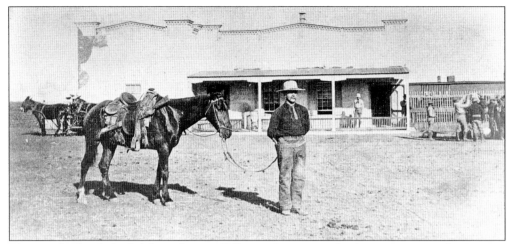

The Brophy family hailed from County Kilkenny. James was the first to arrive in the Arizona Territory. He had joined his brother Thomas in Australia, sailed to Peru, and then went on to San Francisco. James established a ranch in the Sulphur Springs Valley at Soldier's Watering Hole. With water, but no cattle, he sold to the Chiricahua Cattle Company. James is pictured here at the Chiricahua Ranch. The army troops in the background are on maneuvers searching for Geronimo. James spent 11 years in San Diego, returning to Bisbee and opening the Brophy Carriage Company in Lowell, as well as purchasing a ranch in Sulphur Springs Valley. (Arizona Historical Society/Tucson #15933.)

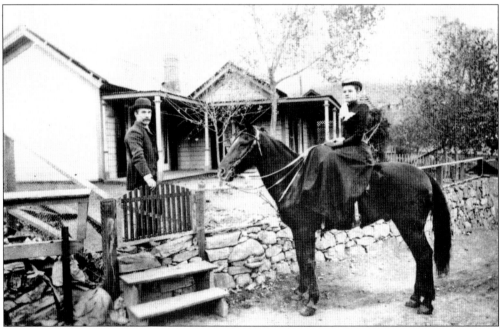

William Brophy arrived from Ireland to join James at his ranch in 1881. Not taking to life as a cowboy, he moved to Bisbee and worked at Mary Crossey's store. The Copper Queen Mining Company needed a store and purchased Crossey's with the condition William went with it. Later, parallel to his career with the Phelps Dodge Corporation, William became a banker and man of affairs. William and his wife, Ellen Goodbody, are pictured in Bisbee in 1892. (Arizona Historical Society/Tucson #15942.)

William Brophy was involved in banking in Arizona, Texas, and California. In the 1920s, states like Arizona saw a drop in the raw commodities of cattle and copper. Through his banking interests, William laid the groundwork to prevent financial disaster for Arizona. William went to France in 1917 to serve the United States in the American Red Cross. He served as chief of stores in charge of Red Cross supply distribution in Western Europe. (Stephen Brophy.)

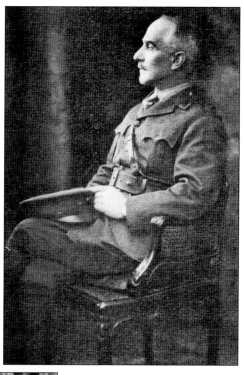

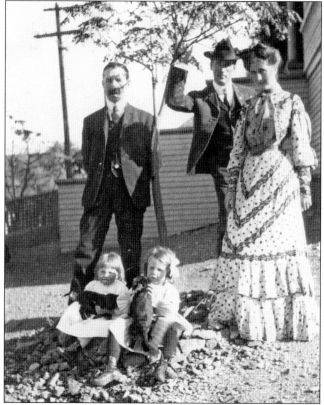

Michael Brophy joined his brothers in Bisbee. He and William prospered as merchants, bankers, and mining men. In 1900, they organized a company to distribute power and ice to Bisbee and developed a localized telephone service. The two brothers were also involved with the construction of the Gadsden Hotel in Douglas. Pictured here are, from left to right, (first row) daughters Helen and Mary; (second row) Michael, brother-in-law Ed Flanigan, and wife Sabina. (Stephen Brophy.)

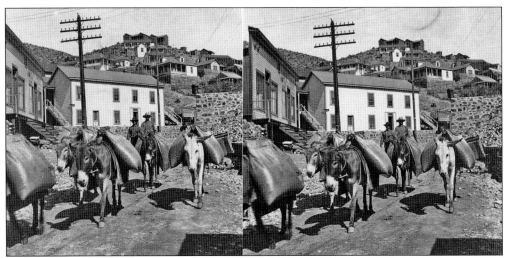

Michael Brophy started a water delivery service for Bisbee. He had a well in Tombstone Canyon and a herd of burros that made deliveries from canvas water sacks. Later, Michael, William, and a group of associates bought Naco Wells and put in a modern water system, probably the most expensive water in the United States, pumped 9 miles and lifted over 2,000 feet. (Arizona Historical Foundation.)

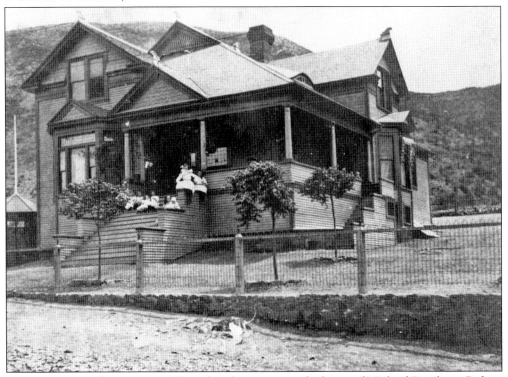

A children's birthday party is celebrated in this picture at the home of Michael Brophy in Bisbee. A fourth Brophy brother, Thomas, arrived in the territory in later years. He had been involved in an abortive Republican movement and was forced to leave Ireland without delay. He spent 40 years in Australia, South America, and the United States before joining his brothers in Arizona. (Stephen Brophy.)

Michael J. Cunningham was born in San Francisco and moved to Tombstone at an early age. He was raised by his aunt Nellie Cashman after the death of his parents, Thomas and Frances (Cashman) Cunningham. Michael was cashier of the Bank of Bisbee and elected to the board of directors. He also served as director of the Bank of Douglas and the Douglas Investment Company, as well as president of the Arizona Banker's Association. His wife, Mary Goodbody, was the sister of Mrs. William Brophy (Ellen). (*Who's Who in Arizona*, 1913.)

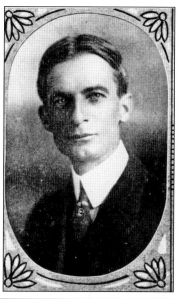

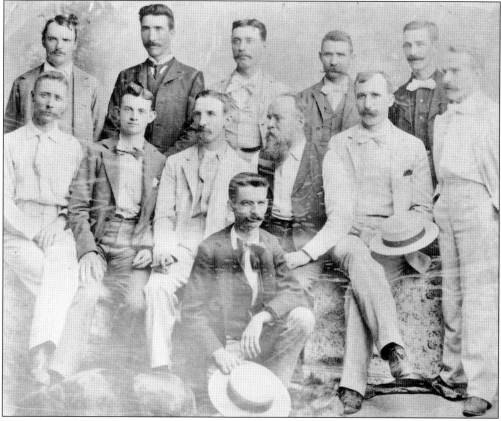

Pictured are the heads of various departments of the Copper Queen store in Bisbee. From left to right are (first row) Michael Cunningham; (second row) Steve Miller, B. J. O'Reilly, Michael Brophy, L. L. Brown, John Campbell, and William Brophy; (third row) Alex Kier, Angus Campbell, A. R. McLeod, Jim Buckley, and Frank Johnson. (Arizona Historical Society/Tucson #14300.)

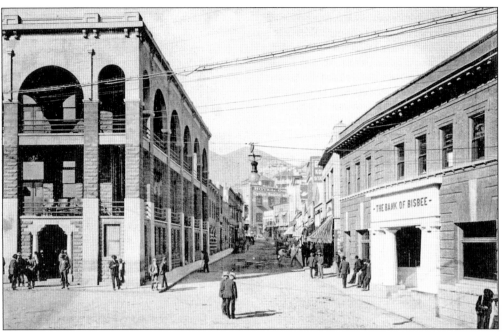

William Brophy organized the Bank of Bisbee in 1900 with Nellie Cashman's nephew, M. J. Cunningham, as cashier. The Bank of Bisbee was the only bank on the Mexican border between El Paso and Tucson. Two years later, the Copper Queen moved the smelter from Bisbee to the Sulphur Springs Valley. Brophy and Cunningham organized the Bank of Douglas in the new city. (Arizona Historical Foundation.)

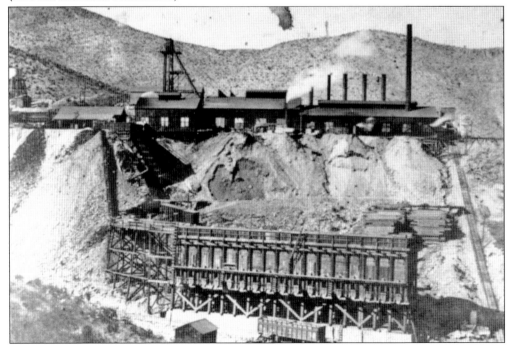

The Irish Mag Mine is viewed from Buckey O'Neill Hill. The mine is said to have been named for an Irish "lady of the evening." (Bisbee Mining and Historical Society #1.1.140.)

Underground mining was a hazardous occupation. The first highly skilled Western miners were "Cousin Jacks" from Cornwall. They were followed by Irish laborers. Initially, the two groups did not get along, as they brought their old methods, ideas, and Protestant/Catholic hatreds with them. Later the workers adapted and joined each other in celebration of St. George and St. Patrick's Days. These Bisbee miners had only candlelight to work by deep down in the mine. (Bisbee Mining and Historical Society #74.53.36.)

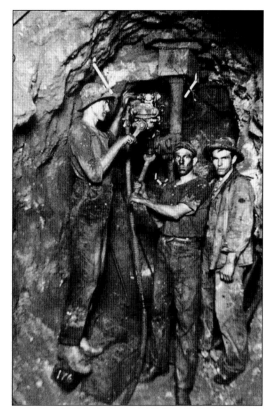

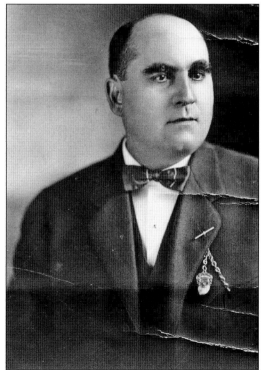

James Letson arrived from Ireland at age 14, poor and illiterate. He made his way to Missouri, where he worked on a farm. At age 23, he arrived in New Mexico and eventually reached the Golden Rule mining camp in Arizona. Letson worked hauling mining equipment from Tombstone to Mexico and was elected constable of Fairbanks. (Glen Peterson.)

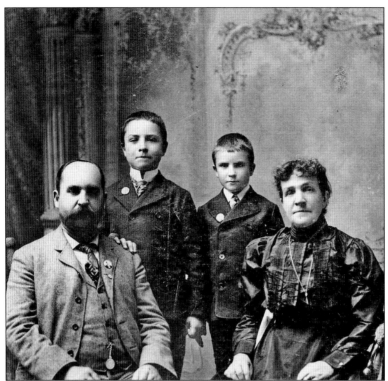

James Letson settled in Bisbee and married a widow, Maggie Madigan Dohoney, from County Clare. The couple is pictured with their sons, James Jr. (left) and John (right). Maggie was a very successful businesswoman in her own right and owned a number of properties in Bisbee. (Glen Peterson.)

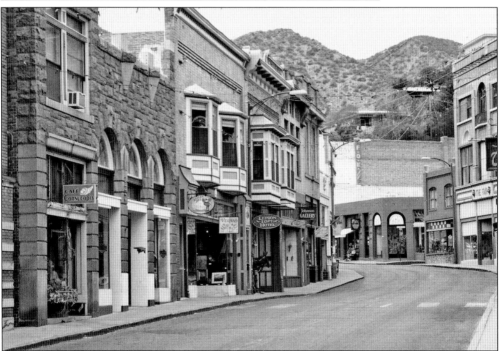

Three years after opening the Clark and Letson saloon, James and Maggie Letson invested in land and the cattle business in the Bisbee area. After Bisbee's 1888 fire, the Letson block was built. The building is now recognized as one of the oldest brick structures in the city. (Glen Peterson.)

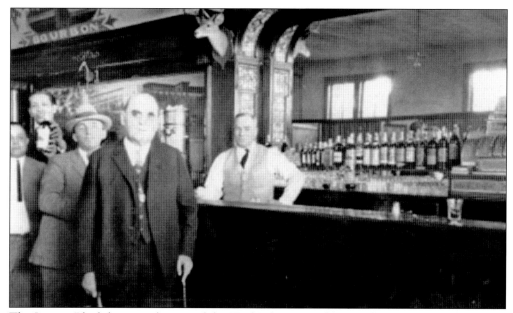

The Letson Block became the site of the Turf Saloon. In addition, the Letsons purchased the Mansion House, the Bisbee camp's most elegant hotel. James is pictured with customers in the Turf. The *Daily Review* noted "the fixtures in the saloon are especially fine, the bar being expensive and elegant, costing over $1,500." (Glen Peterson.)

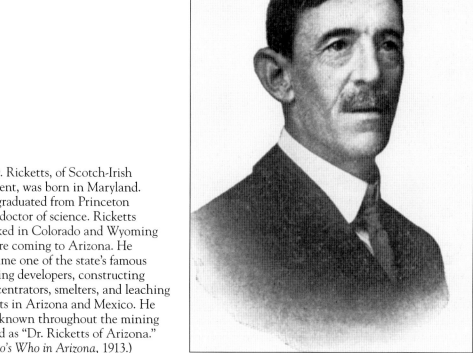

L. D. Ricketts, of Scotch-Irish descent, was born in Maryland. He graduated from Princeton as a doctor of science. Ricketts worked in Colorado and Wyoming before coming to Arizona. He became one of the state's famous mining developers, constructing concentrators, smelters, and leaching plants in Arizona and Mexico. He was known throughout the mining world as "Dr. Ricketts of Arizona." (*Who's Who in Arizona*, 1913.)

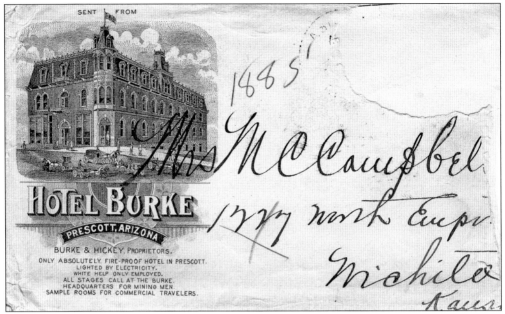

Hotel Burke was built in 1880 at the corner of Montezuma and Gurley Streets in Prescott. Proprietors were Dennis A. Burke and Michael J. Hickey. Hickey was born in 1853 in County Clare. He came to Arizona in 1879 as a miner and became deputy sheriff under Buckey O'Neill in 1882. Hickey was described in 1896 as "a liberal-hearted, public-spirited citizen, who has great hopes of Arizona's future." (Sharlot Hall Museum.)

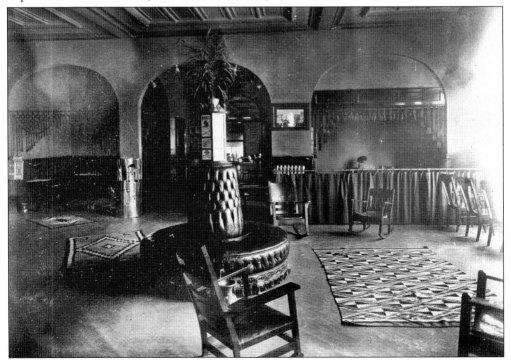

Around 1901, Dennis Burke sold his share of the Burke Hotel to Michael Hickey, who renamed it the Hotel St. Michael. (Arizona Historical Foundation.)

Frank M. Murphy, brother of territorial governor Nathan Oakes Murphy, came to Arizona from Wisconsin in 1877. He was president of the Santa Fe, Prescott, and Phoenix Railroad, which reached Phoenix in 1895. Murphy was cofounder of the Prescott National Bank, and he donated the land for the Prescott Pioneers' Home, certain that "Nowhere in these United States can be found more promising opportunities than are in evidence in Yavapai County." (*Who's Who in Arizona*, 1913.)

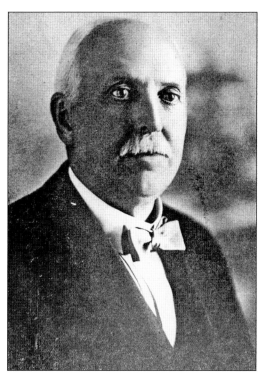

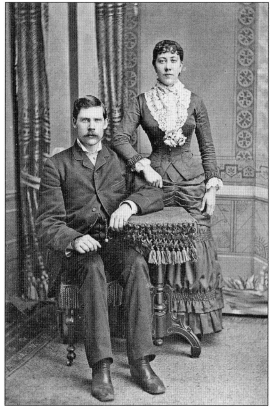

Patrick Fitzgerald was born in Cork, Ireland. He arrived in Prescott in 1871. In the Irish tradition of the day, he started mining in the Turkey Creek/Crown King area of the Bradshaw Mountains. Patrick journeyed to New York City in 1882, where he met Margaret Donohue, daughter of Irish-born parents. They were married in St. Patrick's Cathedral, then under construction, in 1882. (Gladys Mahoney.)

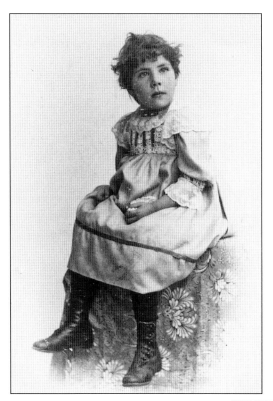

Patrick and Margaret Fitzgerald settled at the mining camp in Turkey Creek, where their first five children were born. Patrick prospected in that remote area, ending up as foreman of the Senator Mine. In 1894, the family moved to Prescott, where five more children were born. Daughter Alice, pictured here, was secretary to Michael Cuniff, who drafted Arizona's constitution. She married William P. Mahoney Sr. in 1915. (Gladys Mahoney.)

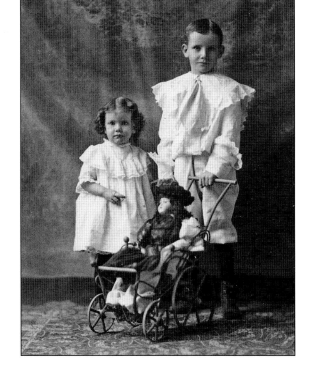

This 1907 photograph of two other Fitzgerald children, Gertrude and Gerald, was taken in Prescott. Families often sent pictures home to Ireland to show relatives how well they were faring in their new homes. (Gladys Mahoney.)

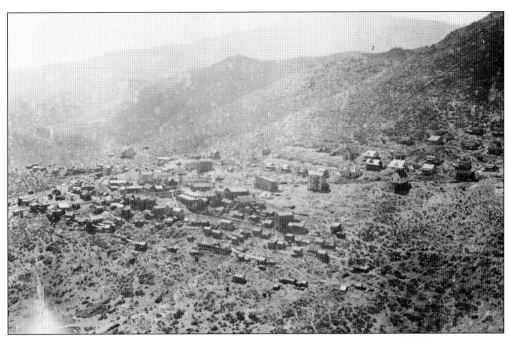

Jerome was built on the east slope of Mingus Mountain and became one of the largest mining towns in the West. (B. W. Bryson.)

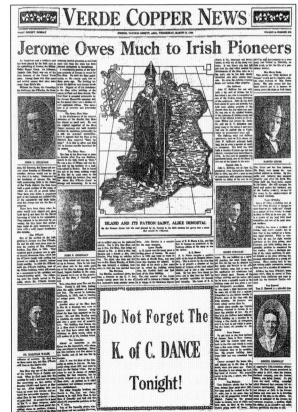

Almost the entire issue of the March 17, 1920, edition of the *Verde Copper News* was given over to stories about the Irish in Jerome and their support for the Republic of Ireland, which was not yet a reality. (Jerome Historical Society.)

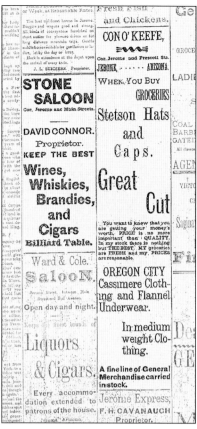

Irish merchants like David O'Connor, Con O'Keefe, and Dan "King" Shea kept Jerome in business, as evidenced in these advertisements from the March 2, 1895, *Jerome Chronicle*. Shea was born in Millstreet, County Cork, Ireland, about 1865 and found his way to Arizona around 1895 as a laborer during the mining boom. He established "Shea's Place," a saloon that was "a quiet and convenient place to spend a spare moment." His Shea Copper Company prospered while Jerome's boom lasted. (Jerome Historical Society.)

Cornelius "Con" O'Keefe was born in Ireland and arrived in New York with his father in 1875. He came to Arizona in 1880, spending time in Yuma, Prescott, and nine years in Jerome. Heading for Mexico, he was involved with several copper companies before selling his interests and moving to Nogales, Arizona. President Roosevelt appointed him collector of the Port of Nogales in 1908, and he was reappointed by President Taft in 1912. His right to hold federal office was questioned, as his father was not an American citizen. The matter was decided in O'Keefe's favor. He married Hannah Shay, and they had four children. Shown here from left to right are (first row) Con and daughter Margaret; (second row) Con Jr., John, and Hannah. Charles, the third son, is not pictured. (*Who's Who in Arizona*, 1913.)

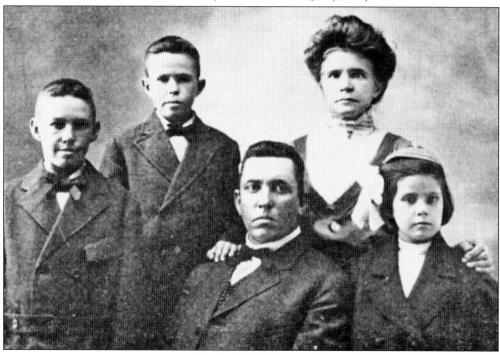

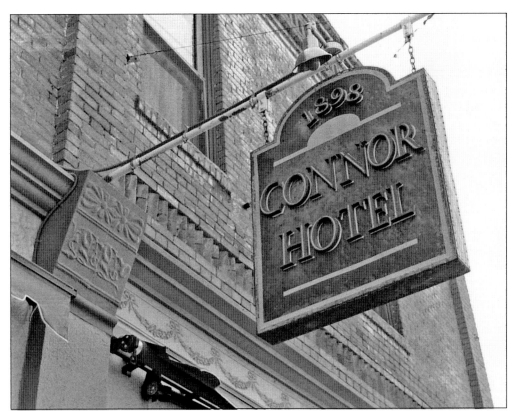

David Connor of Massachusetts moved from Prescott to Jerome in the 1880s as a miner. He built the first stone structure in town, the Stone Saloon, unusual in a place full of temporary wood and canvas shelters. The location burned and was rebuilt six times, eventually rising as the brick Connor Hotel, which still operates as a hotel today. In 1897, rooms were $1 a night. (Kathleen Shappee Wood [KSW].)

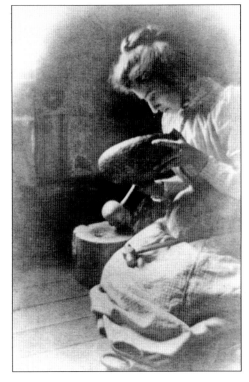

Mary Colter was born in Pittsburgh, Pennsylvania, in 1869 to Irish immigrant parents. She built a reputation as an artist and designer, capitalizing on her love for Native American art and culture. She designed many of the iconic buildings at Grand Canyon Village, including Hopi House, Hermit's Rest, Bright Angel Lodge, Lookout Studio, the Watchtower at Desert View, and Phantom Ranch. (Grand Canyon National Park Museum, Mary Larkin Smith Collection #16952.)

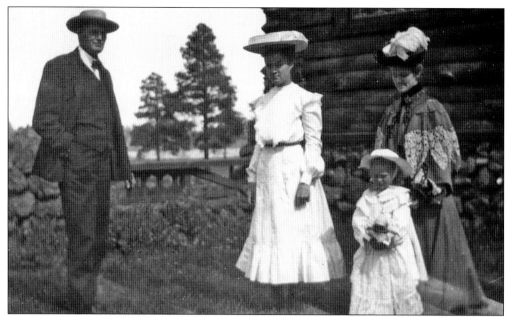

The Riordan brothers, Matt, Tim, and Michael, were middle-class Irish Americans from Chicago, sons of a carpenter who was born in Ireland. Matt Riordan, the oldest son, was born in 1848. He was a Civil War veteran and went west after the war, like many others, looking for opportunity. Matt arrived in Flagstaff in the spring of 1884 to take the position of manager at the Ayer Lumber Company. Three years later, he became the owner. The Arizona Lumber and Timber Company would remain the biggest employer in Flagstaff for the next 40 years. Tim (left) appears here in 1905 with, from left to right, daughters Mary and Anna and wife Caroline. (Riordan Mansion State Historic Park.)

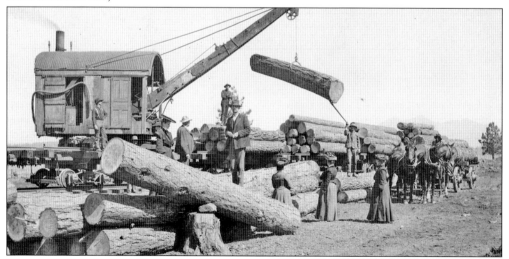

The middle Riordan son, Tim, received an invitation from brother Matt to join him in Flagstaff and help run the mill; he did so in 1886, running daily operations and freeing Matt to negotiate contracts and pursue capital investments. Tim served as the president of the Arizona Lumber and Timber Company until he sold the controlling interest in the lumber company in 1933. Individuals in this picture are unidentified. (Northern Arizona University, Cline Library, Special Collections and Archives, AHS.0020.00194, Colorado Plateau Digital Archives.)

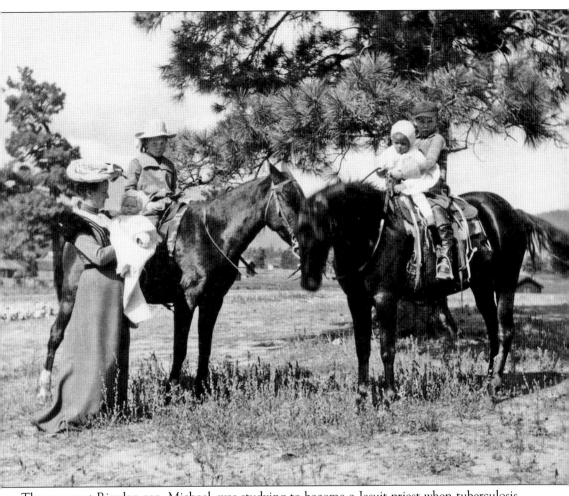

The youngest Riordan son, Michael, was studying to become a Jesuit priest when tuberculosis ended his academic career. Matt invited Michael to join him in Flagstaff to recover his health and help him run the business; Michael did so in 1885. He became secretary of the company and held that position until his death in 1930. Michael wrote extensively; he sent his poetry, editorials, and articles to publications all over the country, and he did not shy away from taking on controversial topics. He traveled all over the world, including to Ireland; his scrapbooks, archived at the Cline Library at Northern Arizona University, include a hand-written note from Éamon de Valera, the president of the Irish Republic, declining the audience Michael sought with him on one of his visits. Pictured in 1904 are, from left to right, Michael's wife, Elizabeth, holding son Robert; daughter Blanche; daughter Clare; and son Arthur on horseback. (Riordan Mansion State Historic Park.)

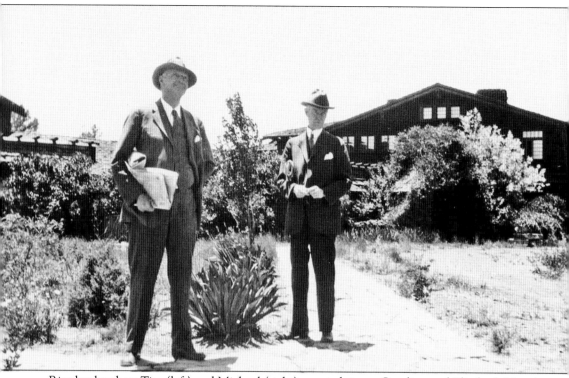

Riordan brothers Tim (left) and Michael (right) married sisters Caroline and Elizabeth Metz in 1889 and 1892, respectively. The women were cousins of the Babbitts, another prominent Arizona family. In July 1902, the Riordans met Charles Whittlesey, chief architect for the Santa Fe Railway, who was in the process of designing a grand hotel at the Grand Canyon. Michael suggested the name "El Tovar" for the hotel, based on his interest in Spanish explorers in the American West. Tim and Michael, by now well-established and prosperous businessmen, hired Whittlesey to design a large home to be shared by their two growing families. Construction began on the adjoining houses in November 1903, and the families moved in by September 1904. The homes, built and furnished in the American Arts and Crafts style, included a total of 13,000 square feet of living space and progressive new features for the times, like hot and cold running water, central heat, and electric lights. The grounds and the homes are open to the public as Riordan Mansion State Historic Park. (Riordan Mansion State Historic Park.)

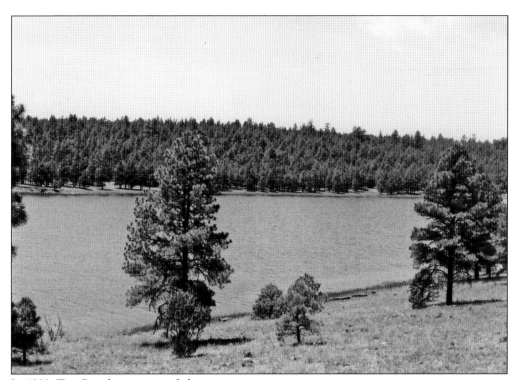

In 1903, Tim Riordan conceived the idea of building a lake south of Flagstaff, naming it Mary in honor of his daughter. The lake became an important factor in Flagstaff's municipal water supply. (Kelly Bryant.)

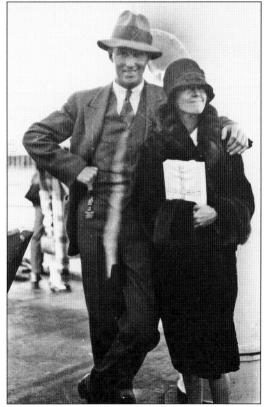

An exile from Ireland found his way to Flagstaff in the 1920s. William Quirke had been active in political and military affairs in Ireland during the Irish Civil War; he left for America possibly to lie low until the political situation at home cooled down. He located the Riordans, who employed him at Arizona Lumber and Timber. While he was there, he met and married Michael Riordan's daughter Clare, taking her back to Ireland to live permanently. Michael, always interested in Ireland and Irish affairs, visited the couple at their home. (Riordan Mansion State Historic Park.)

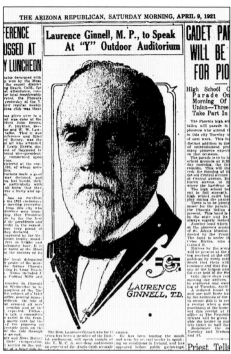

Laurence Ginnell was an outspoken anti-landlord activist in his native Ireland in the early 1900s. He was elected to the first Dáil Éireann (Irish Parliament) in 1918 and toured America in 1921 to raise money and support for the Irish Republic. Ginnell spoke in Tucson on April 7, 1921, and Phoenix on April 9. He also visited the home of Michael Riordan in Flagstaff. (Phoenix Public Library, the Arizona Republican Microfilm Archives.)

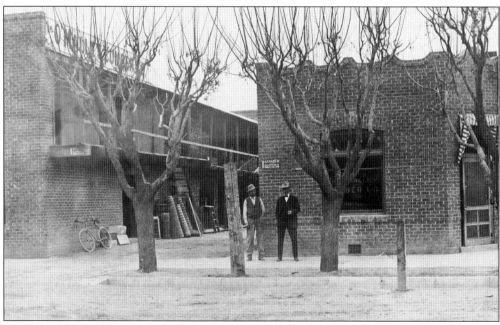

Edward and James O'Malley, born in County Mayo and raised in Scotland, were drawn to America to join relatives in St. Louis. After much hard work, they purchased a lumber company in Missouri in 1877. Joined by other family members, the O'Malleys expanded to other states. James married Kate Malone, and in 1908, their sons learned the DeMund Lumber Company in Phoenix was for sale. Edward, John, and Charles believed there was potential in the raw frontier of Arizona. This 1908 photograph shows the original O'Malley lumberyard in Phoenix. The individuals are not identified. (Arizona State University, Hayden Library, Hayden Collection #CPFIB 20.1.)

This O'Malley's advertisement appeared in a supplement of the *Arizona Republic* celebrating Arizona's 50th anniversary in 1962. (*Arizona Republic*, Arizona Days and Ways 50th anniversary issue, 1962.)

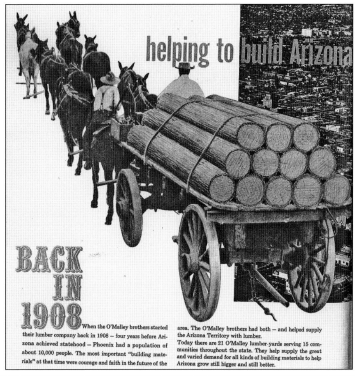

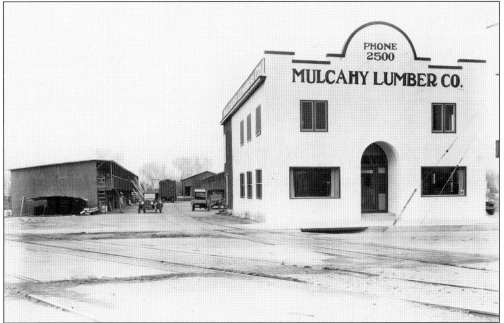

John Mulcahy was born in Canada, his father having immigrated there from Ireland. Coming to Arizona in 1913, he was associated with Kelvin Lumber in Winkelman. In 1923, Mulcahy was manager of the Tucson branch of O'Malley Lumber. He and Alfred Paul organized Mulcahy Lumber Company with the purchase of the John W. Rush Lumber Company. Gov. R. C. Stanford appointed Mulcahy to the Colorado River Commission. (Arizona Historical Society/Tucson #10435.)

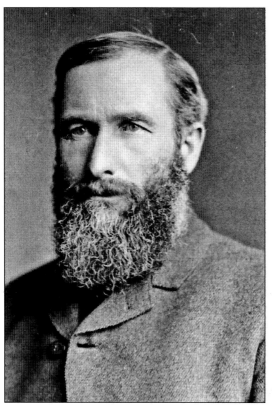

William John Murphy was born in New Hartford, New York, in 1839, although his parents and two older siblings were born in Dunane, County Antrim, in Northern Ireland. After a varied career, he became a railroad-grading contractor and went west with the railroad, moving his wife and six children to Arizona in 1881. The family came to Phoenix in 1883 when Murphy took a contract to build the Arizona Canal in the Salt River Valley. (Glendale Historical Society.)

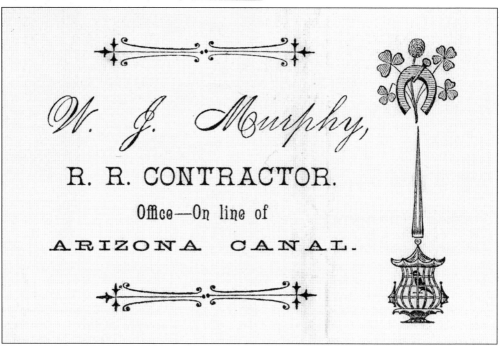

Murphy's business letterhead of 1883 shows a connection to his Irish heritage. (Arizona State University Library, Hayden Collection.)

W. J. Murphy's wife, Laura (seated at right), lived in a tent by the canal with the six children for two years during construction. Murphy traveled around the United States and to England and Scotland to sell bonds to finance the work, since his contract called for payment in bonds rather than cash. His efforts promoted long-term water planning, agricultural pioneering, and public transportation across the region. He constructed Grand Avenue from Phoenix to the site of Glendale, which he promoted as a temperance colony. (Glendale Historical Society.)

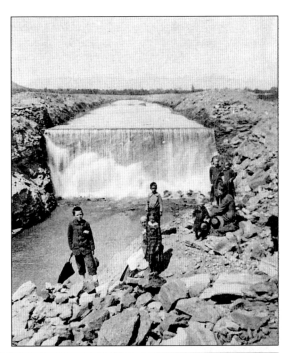

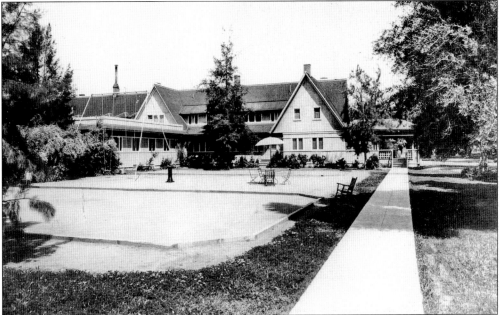

Murphy's vision for the region blossomed at Ingleside in Phoenix, a tract of land on which he built the Ingleside Inn, pictured here in 1910, and planted orange and other fruit trees; ash and olive trees were planted along the streets. The inn and cottages served as a private club for potential investors and property buyers. There was a desert golf course with an oiled sand surface in an area that could not be irrigated. Only the name, Ingleside, remains in area schools and businesses. The Murphy Bridle Path—an unpaved, shaded path bordering Central Avenue—is a reminder of the dirt road Murphy graded as the original Central Avenue. (Arizona Historical Foundation, Creighton Collection.)

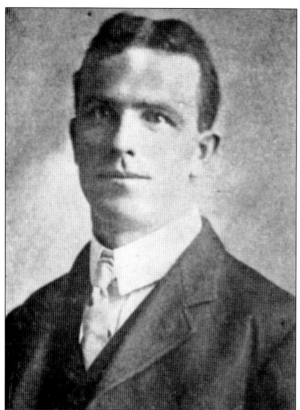

Peter Sullivan came to Phoenix in 1900. He served on the police force, with double duty for a time as fire chief and police officer. During his service, the Adams Hotel was consumed by fire. Sullivan's ability, sound judgment, and management kept the fire confined, and it did not spread to adjacent buildings. Shortly after the fire, he was appointed as chief of the Phoenix Fire Department. (*Who's Who in Arizona*, 1913.)

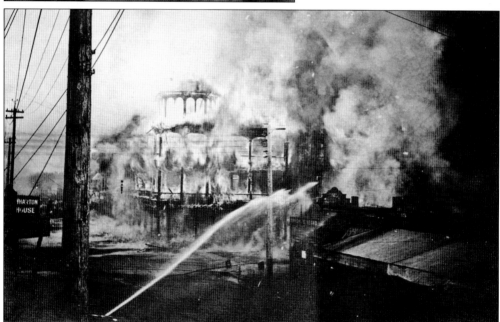

The Adams Hotel in Phoenix was legendary. The original hotel was a massive 200-room building erected in 1896. A wooden structure, it burned in a spectacular fire in May 1910. (Arizona Historical Foundation.)

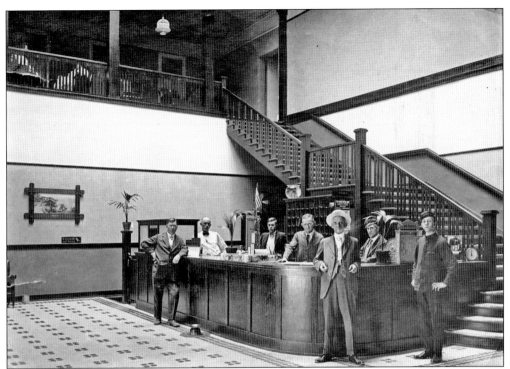

Thomas Devine's parents were from Ireland and were early pioneers in Michigan. He came to Arizona and took a position with the railroad in Flagstaff. Devine was elected treasurer of Coconino County. Moving to Mohave County, he purchased the Beale Hotel in Kingman and was elected treasurer of Mohave County. The Beale Hotel lobby is shown here; the men are unidentified. (Mohave County Historical Society #4025.)

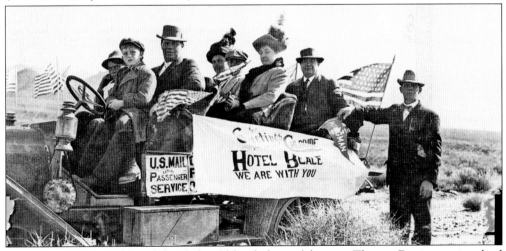

The Devine family and friends headed to Chloride for a celebration. Thomas Devine was involved with the Good Roads Association, a group of Northern Arizona citizens who successfully had the National Old Trails Highway take the northern route through Arizona rather than the southern route. The highway became famous as Route 66. Passengers are, from left to right, Ted Bland, Andy Devine, Tom Devine, Amy Devine, Tom Devine Jr., Lucy Conant, Martin Hamilton, and Jack Fettus. (Mohave County Historical Society #1517.)

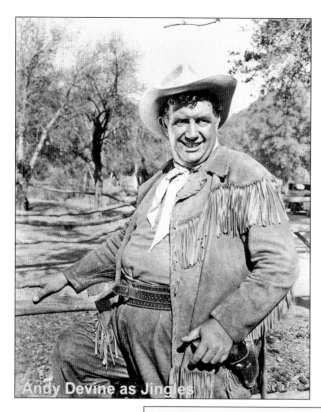

Thomas and Amy Devine's sons, Tom and Andy, worked in the Beale Hotel for their father. Andy was standing on a street corner in Hollywood when he was "discovered." He made over 400 film, radio, stage, and television appearances, including playing Jingles, sidekick to Wild Bill Hickok. (Mohave County Historical Society #6678.)

Michael Rice was born in Ireland; orphaned, he was sent to an aunt in San Francisco, California. After a long voyage around Cape Horn, he arrived in California, then headed for Arizona. Returning to San Francisco, he met Pauline Cushman, the famous Union spy. Rice was her bellboy and servant and became like a brother to her. He traveled with Cushman and her husband to Florence, where he worked as a newspaper reporter. (Pinal County Historical Society.)

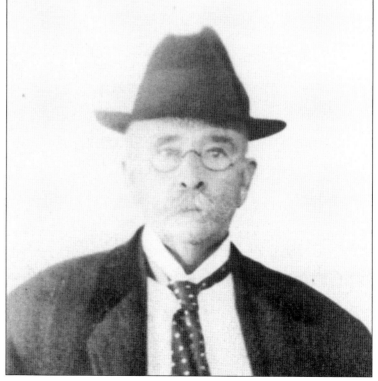

Tom McAuliff came to Florence from Ireland in 1901. He was a stonemason and prospector. At the time of this 1933 picture, he still had claims in the Mineral Hill District. The *Arizona Blade Tribune* noted that he was one of the most skillful brick and stonemasons in the county. (Pinal County Historical Society.)

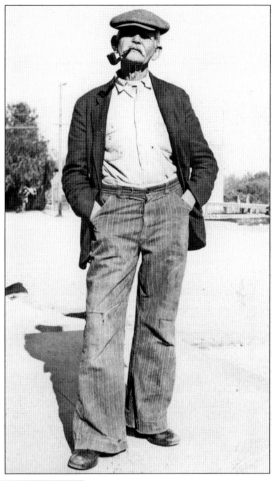

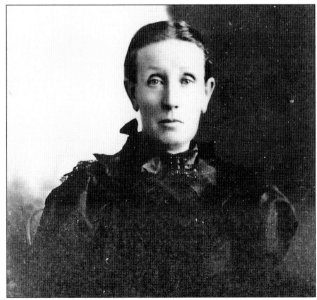

Mary Agnes Clark was born July 15, 1850, in Dublin, Ireland, to Catherine Mullen and Joseph Clark. Her father sailed to America when she was two. Mary's mother died when she was five; she was raised and educated in a Catholic convent. At age 16, she traveled alone to Boston, Massachusetts, where she met and married William H. Perry. Together they moved to Arizona and settled near Cordes on the Agua Fria River. They raised nine children. (Lisa Perry and Gina Ragsdale.)

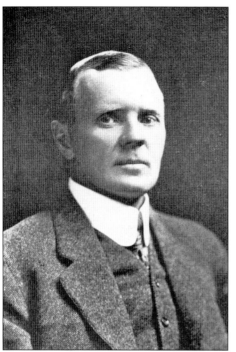

Norman Carmichael was born in Belfast in 1869. He came to the United State and became engaged in mining engineering. After working in British Columbia, Carmichael returned to Arizona in 1905 to become mine superintendent of the Arizona Copper Company in Clifton/Morenci. He was later appointed general manager. (*Who's Who in Arizona*, 1913.)

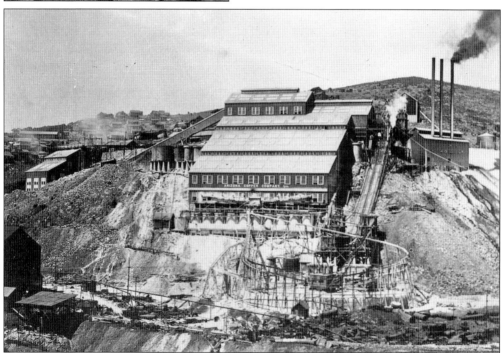

The Arizona Copper Company's lands consisted of about 4,000 acres, containing eight producing mines in Greenlee County. The company was organized in 1884 under the laws of Great Britain, with about 20 percent of company stock in the United States. The main office of the company was located in Edinburgh, Scotland, with the mine and works office in Clifton. (Arizona Historical Foundation.)

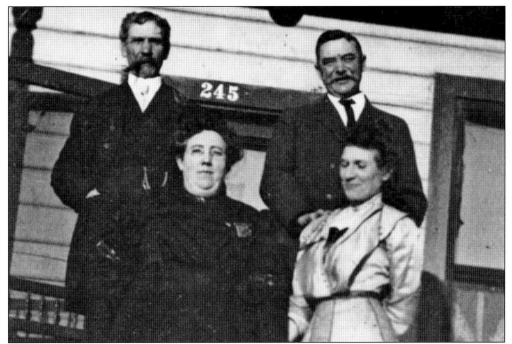

Pictured are, from left to right, (first row) Margaret Murphy and Elizabeth Gleeson; (second row) Denis Murphy and John Gleeson. John Gleeson emigrated from County Tipperary in 1879. He married Elizabeth Cummings, also from Ireland, in 1889. Gleeson prospected all over the West, settling in Cochise County, where he prospected and Elizabeth ran a boardinghouse. Gleeson located the Copper Belle deposit, which proved to be a heavy copper-producing mine, on an older mining claim near Turquoise. (JRB.)

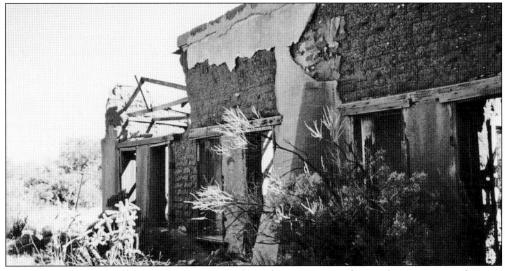

Around 1900, the Turquoise camp was moved to a lower site in order to obtain a more adequate water supply. The new location was named Gleeson, after John. By 1909, the town had 500 people. World War I and the demand for copper helped boost Gleeson's economy. As the years passed, however, Gleeson became a has-been mining town, with the ruins of adobe walls remaining to remind people of its existence. (JRB.)

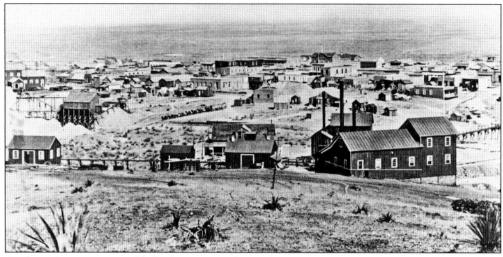

Cochise County was established in 1881 with Tombstone as its seat. Ninety-six hundred people lived in the county, 5,300 in Tombstone. The census listed 2,880 American, 559 Irish, and 279 English, among other nationalities. Hundreds of the Americans listed were of Irish origin. The *Tombstone Epitaph* noted, "The Irish are the least clannish of the foreigners and mix indiscriminately with other peoples, while the English almost invariably live together." (Arizona Historical Society/Tucson #42005.)

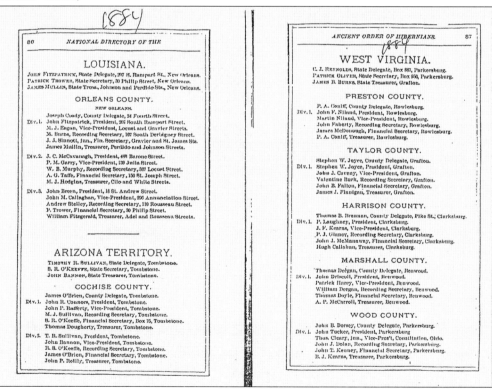

The Irish in Arizona did not typically have time for Irish-oriented service or social organizations. There were exceptions though; the 1884 National Directory of the Ancient Order of Hibernians shows several members on the roster for Tombstone. (Ancient Order of Hibernians of America, Inc.)

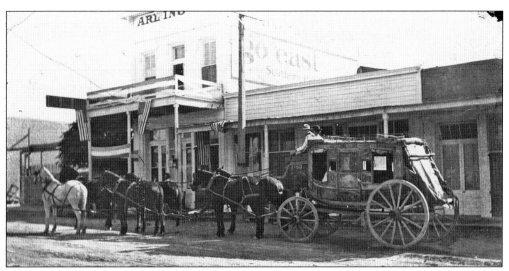

Passengers traveling to Tombstone could go as far as Benson on the train and then take this coach to Tombstone. The coach ride was jolting, hot, and dusty. Stage companies often carried company payrolls, making them a target for robberies. The Butterfield Overland Stage passengers bound for Arizona were issued a warning: "The safety of your person cannot be vouchsafed by anyone but God." (Arizona Historical Foundation, McClintock Collection.)

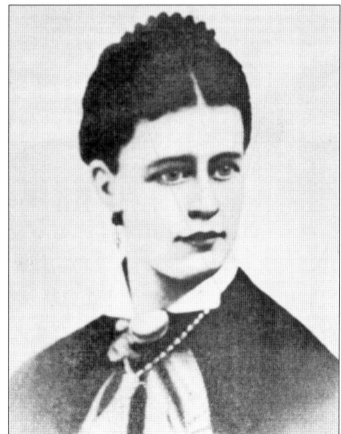

Born Ellen O'Kissane in County Cork, Nellie Cashman met Horace Greeley in Boston and took his advice to "go West." Nellie, her mother, and sister went to San Francisco, then to Nevada, where Nellie opened a boardinghouse. Nellie came to Tucson in 1878, then headed for Tombstone. She was known as the "Angel of Tombstone," giving much of her wealth to needy prospectors, frontier hospitals, and church missions. (Arizona Historical Foundation.)

THE RUSS HOUSE!

MISS NELLIE CASHMAN, Manager.

Thoroughly Refitted   Everything New

Eastern Waiters.   White Cooks.

MEALS 25 CENTS AND UPWARDS.

Board $6.00 per Week, in Advance. $6.50, if Paid Monthly.

Nellie advertised her Tombstone restaurant in the *Tombstone Epitaph*. She was active in community affairs in Tombstone and raised money to build a Catholic church. Tombstone's Schieffelin Hall was inaugurated on March 17, 1881, with a St. Patrick's Day ball as a fund-raiser for the Irish Land League. By the end of 1881, the Irish in Tombstone donated $200 toward the land league. (*Tombstone Epitaph*, March 1882.)

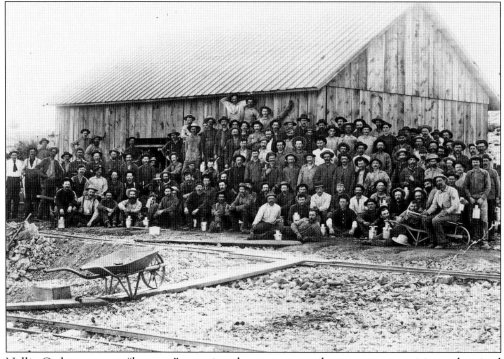

Nellie Cashman was a "boomer," meaning she was attracted to new communities and arrived early on the scene. She traveled around the West and into Mexico, British Columbia, and Alaska. Pictured are employees of the Buffalo Mine near Globe, who were able to stay at the hotel and restaurant Nellie opened near the mine in January 1896. (Arizona State Library, History and Archives Division/Phoenix #96.4498.)

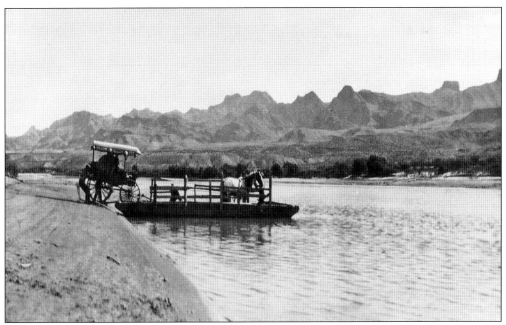

The Grand Gulch Trail was named for the Grand Gulch Mine north of the Colorado River. One fork of the trail went through the Scanlon Dugway, a treacherous trail for any freighter. The trail ended at the Scanlon Ferry on the Colorado River, owned by Irishman Mike Scanlon. (Phoenix Public Library, Arizona Room #7:94.)

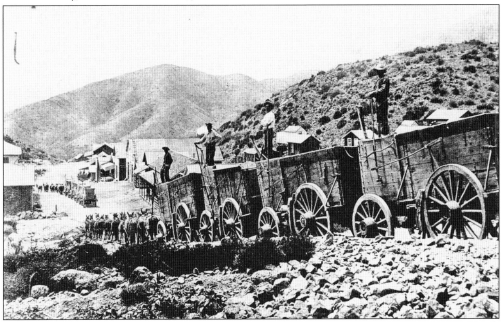

In 1882, the Silver King mine was producing large amounts of ore, and the community prospered. The first ore from the mine was shipped to San Francisco for smelting. A mill was later erected at Pinal, and 20-mule teams hauled wagons of ore to Pinal for processing. Silver King was abandoned in 1888, when the silver price plummeted. Voting records show a number of Irish in the community. (Arizona Historical Foundation.)

Alice Donovan Curnow left Nevada to join her husband, Tom, at a mining camp in Richmond Basin in 1881. The couple lived in a tent home, and the women and children would hide in a tunnel when the Apaches were about. Later moving to Mesa and Tempe, Tom operated successful repair shops with his skill at carpentry and blacksmithing, as well as his mechanical expertise. (Arizona Historical Society/Tucson #8172.)

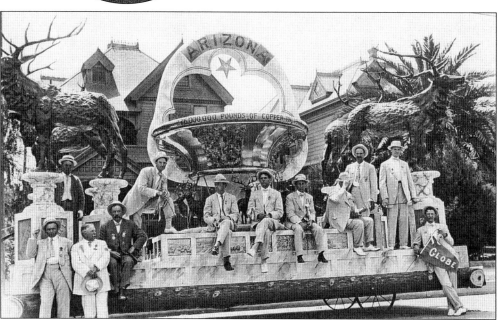

John J. Maloney was active in the Globe Elks; his photo album included a picture of unidentified members of the Globe Elks with their float for an Arizona Elks Convention parade. The Irish in Arizona were not often able to create organizations typical of larger Irish American populations. The Benevolent and Protective Order of Elks was very popular with the Irish all over the state. Other organizations included the Knights of Columbus, Knights of Pythias, International Order of Odd Fellows, and Moose and Masonic Lodges. (JRB.)

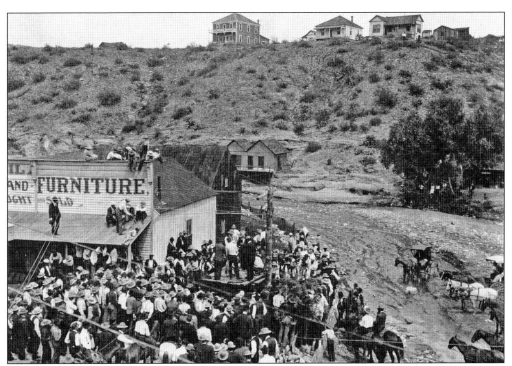

Communities were often isolated, and citizens were responsible for their own entertainment. Pictured here is a drilling contest for miners in Globe. Territorial newspapers reported on baseball games, horse races, town band concerts, and balls where citizens danced until the wee hours of the morning. A St. Patrick's ball was held each year in a number of communities, such as Globe, Tombstone, and Jerome. (JRB.)

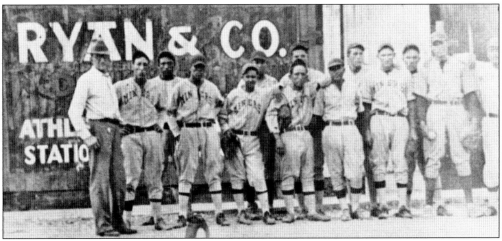

William Ryan was known as a fanatic baseball fan. At the urging of brother-in-law John Moloney, Ryan and Company began stocking athletic equipment in 1907. Unidentified players and a coach for the Globe Miners team are pictured around 1910 in front of a Ryan and Company billboard at the ball park in Globe. Part of the Globe St. Patrick's Day celebration in 1890 was a baseball game—Old Dominion versus the "town boys." Before either side had scored a point, the ball burst and was stuffed with rags to continue the game, which was won by the "boys." (Gila County Historical Society.)

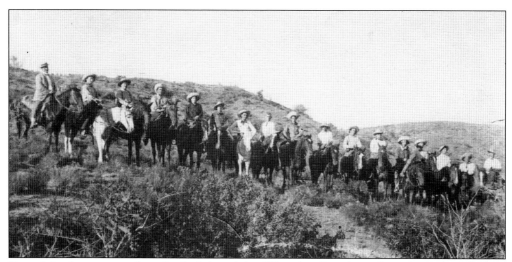

Denis Murphy is pictured on the far left with his Wineglass Ranch cowboys. Denis branded the wineglass on cattle at his ranch, located 12 miles east of Casadore Springs in Gila County. He wanted his cowboys to ride the sorriest horses into town. Denis didn't want any of his good horses stolen when they were tied to the hitching rails outside of the Globe Saloons. (JRB.)

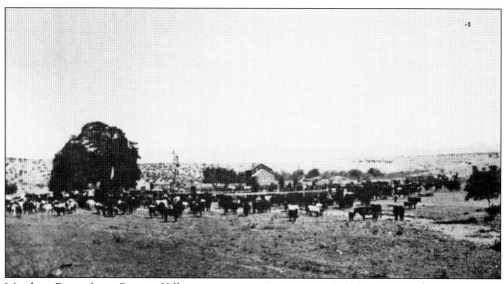

Matthew Ryan, from County Kilkenny, came to America at 13. He was an Irish success story, with shops, packinghouses, mercantile stores, and ranches in Kansas and Wyoming. In 1894, sons Matthew Jr., Jeptha, and Thomas ventured into ranching in Arizona. The 4-Bar Headquarters was located near Soldier's Hole in Cochise County. Following a drought and the loss of land due to settlers, the brothers moved to Colorado in 1903. (Mary Magoffin.)

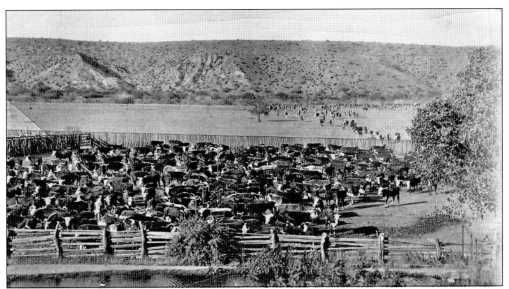

William and Anna Ryan's sons, William Albert, Cornelius, Edward Emmet, and Joseph, ranched on the Apache reservation. The Apaches decided to go into the cattle business themselves and were not renewing leases. No buyers wanted cattle in the Depression. The Ryan brothers moved their cattle to the Five Slash Ranch they purchased on the Salt River. Their cattle are shown being driven to the Cross S Corrals near Globe. (JRB.)

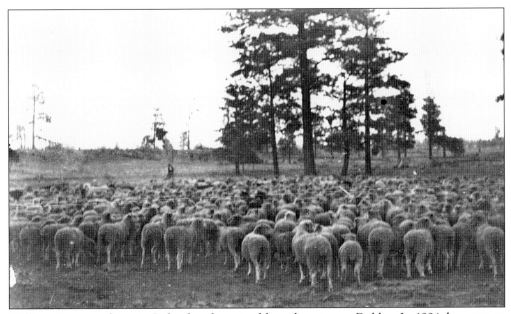

William Dagg was born in Ireland and received his education in Dublin. In 1884, he came to the United States, arriving in Winslow in 1885 for his health. Dagg bought and later sold the Cass and Tuft Mercantile. He moved to his sheep ranch in Navajo County, owned with Mr. Rand. This picture is representative of the area near the Dagg and Rand sheep ranch. Dagg later returned to Winslow and bought back the mercantile company. (Phoenix Public Library, Arizona Room #9.3.)

Dan Mooney, a red-headed Irishman, was in an 1882 prospecting party to Havasu Canyon that included Edward L. Doheny, who later struck oil in California. The search for minerals led to a risky effort to climb down a cliff face near a waterfall; Mooney fell to his death, and the falls have borne his name ever since. Doheny remarked, "Mooney was very reckless, and did not exercise the caution that 100 percent sanity would dictate." (Phoenix Public Library, Arizona Room #7:25.)

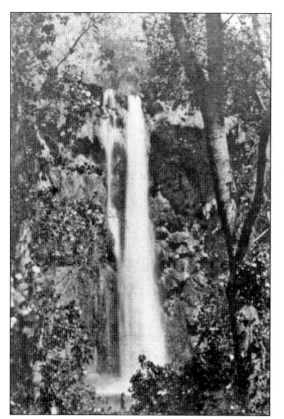

Al Doyle (right) served as wilderness guide to Sharlot Hall (center), John Muir, and Zane Grey in Northern Arizona. He was born in Detroit, Michigan, in 1849 and came to Flagstaff in 1872. Doyle's experience and reputation made it possible for Sharlot Hall to introduce the Arizona Strip to the rest of the world. Maj. A. J. Doran (left) introduced legislation to create the Pioneers' Home in Prescott. (Sharlot Hall Museum.)

Sara Arizona Dugan was born on July 4, 1881, on the immigrant ship SS *Arizona*. The Dugans, originally from County Clare, immigrated to Glasgow, Scotland, before coming to America. The family came to Gallup, New Mexico, and Sara later attended the Catholic high school in Prescott. After graduation, she was a page in the territorial government. Moving to Winslow at 18, she met Frank Krentz. They married and moved to Douglas to open a butcher shop and raise cattle on the Spear E Ranch. (Rob and Sue Krentz.)

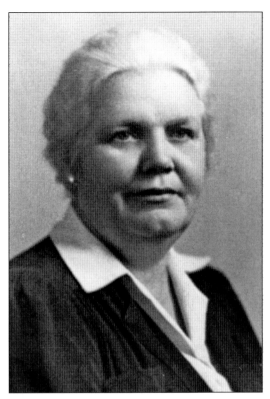

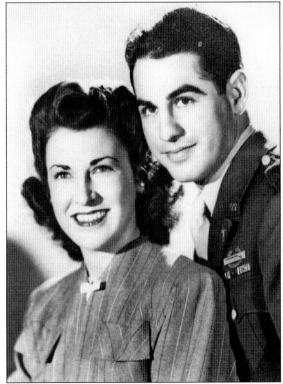

Teresa Savinsky O'Haco was born at West Point Military Academy. Her Czechoslovakian father, Daniel, was a soldier there. Her mother, Catherine Griffin, was from County Cork. Terry graduated from nursing school in 1944 and joined the Army Nurse Corps. At school, an Ouija board told her she would marry a cowboy. Transferred to California, one of her patients was Capt. Mike O'Haco from Winslow. Wounded at Nuremberg, Mike recovered, and Terry married her cowboy. O'Haco Ranch is the oldest privately owned ranch in Arizona. (Kathleen O'Haco.)

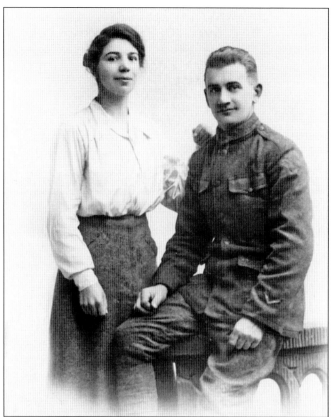

William Thomas McClelland was born in 1891 in Cloughenramer, near Newry, County Down, Ireland. His parents had tenant rights on a farm where they kept 20 cows, as well as sheep, pigs, turkeys, and chickens. In 1912, W. T. "Mr. Mac" McClelland immigrated to America from Northern Ireland, joining an uncle in Tucson. He got work as a ranch hand at the Triple C Ranch in Oracle. In 1920, he brought Sara Winifred "Winnie" Parker from her home in Ballykeel, County Down, and they married in Arizona. (Shamrock Foods.)

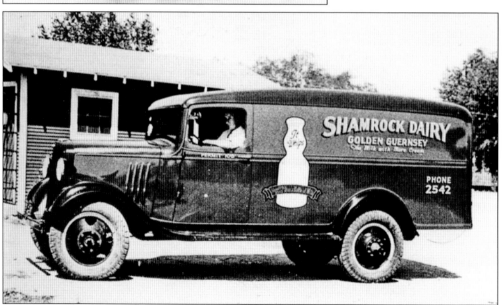

Mr. Mac and his wife, Winnie, founded Shamrock Dairy in Tucson in 1922 with just 20 Guernsey cows, one Model T truck, and a dream. Bill Parker, brother of Winnie Parker McClelland, is behind the wheel. Winnie's mother, Jane Wright, suggested the name Shamrock from the Irish national emblem. (Shamrock Foods.)

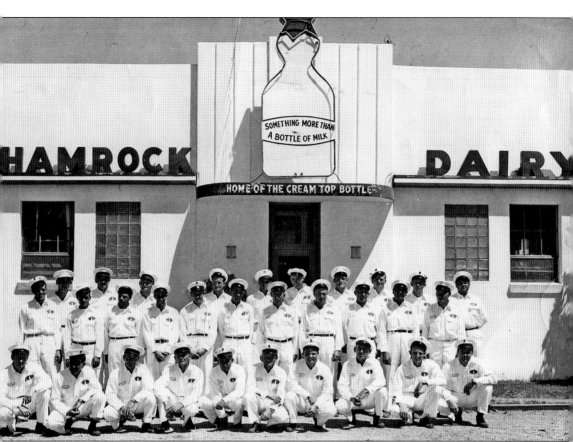

The Shamrock Dairy in Tucson, shown here, continued to grow. In 1956, a new plant was built in Phoenix, and the name changed to Shamrock Foods Company in 1969 to reflect its growth in the food service distribution business. Shamrock Foods Company is still family owned and operated; it includes Shamrock Foods, the seventh-largest food service distributor nationally, and Shamrock Farms, the largest dairy in the Southwest. (Shamrock Foods.)

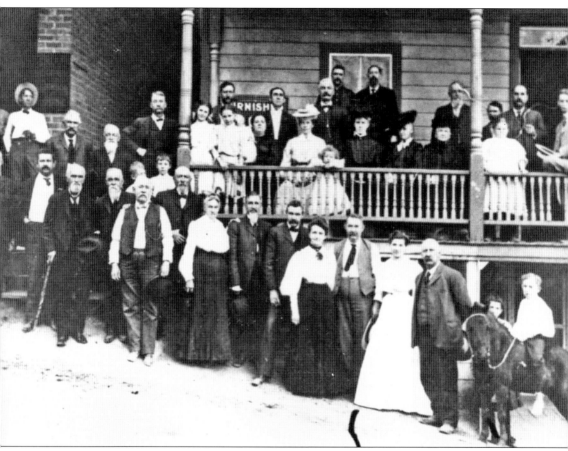

This 1906 photograph shows some of the leading citizens of Bisbee. They are (first row) Martin O'Hara, William Coglin, Mr. Burr, John S. Williams, John Blair, Bill Morris, Mary Walker, Mr. Norton, Peter Johnson, Joe Muirhead, Mrs. Joe Muirhead, James Brophy, and Spencer Clawson on the pony; (second row) unidentified, Dennis Curran, William Tong, I. W. Wallace, Tom Grady, Mrs. Finnalyson, Horace Mann, Mrs. Tom Grady, Charles Strong, Tom Davis, Miss Davis, George Toles, Mrs. Burr, Mrs. Jacob Schmidt, Jacob Schmidt, Henry Manz, Dot Finnalyson, James Letson, and M. J. Cunningham. O'Hara Street was named after Martin. The names do not quite equal all the individuals pictured, and other than Spencer, the children are not identified. (Bisbee Mining and Historical Museum #A93-2380.38.12.)

Three

THE LONG ARM OF THE LAW

The perception of the early American West brings to mind cavalrymen and Native Americans, gunfighters in dusty streets, and the trusty sheriff in his white hat. All these and their families played out their roles in the vast Arizona Territory.

A very small part of the military's time was spent fighting Native Americans. Mostly, they built forts and roads, mapped out the territory, guarded wagon trains and railroad workers, and strung telegraph lines between garrisons. They also assisted in keeping the law, fighting outlaws, bootleggers, and rustlers.

The county sheriff, his deputies, city marshals, town policeman, and the Arizona Rangers maintained law and order, often in isolated areas. Territorial governor Nathan Oakes Murphy established the Arizona Rangers, patterned after the famed Texas Rangers. Although Arizona did have her share of gun battles, most law officers enforced the law without resorting to the use of a gun.

In the early days of the territory, any white male 21 years of age and in good moral character could be admitted to the bar to practice law. Women were admitted in 1892. Those early rules were changed in 1901, creating a better-trained group of legal representatives. Research shows numerous Irish serving at military posts, as law enforcements officers, and as attorneys. There were also a number of Irish politicians and political appointees in our state's history. Could it be they followed the Irish tradition of having the gift of gab?

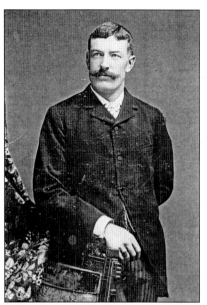

County Tipperary's Jeremiah "Jerry" Ryan found success prospecting and cattle ranching in the Globe area. In 1989, Gila County sheriff Glenn Reynolds appointed Ryan as chief deputy. A warrant was issued for the Apache Kid, and Ryan was sent to intercept him on his way to San Carlos on ration day. The Kid was arrested, tried, and sentenced. He and other Native American prisoners were being escorted to Yuma Territorial Prison when the prisoners overtook the escort, killing Sheriff Reynolds and Deputy Holmes and wounding stage driver Middleton. Ryan was appointed sheriff to finish out Reynolds's term. (JRB.)

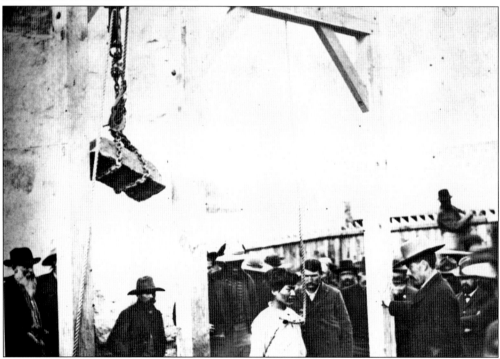

The first "legal" hanging in Globe took place in December 1889. Sheriff Jerry Ryan (without a hat) officiated at the hanging of Nah Diaz, convicted of murdering Lt. Steward Mott of Fort San Carlos. Larry Ball's Desert Lawmen described Ryan's inexperience in hanging his prisoner: "in the dark humor of that day, the victim was 'jerked to Jesus.' Ryan attached too heavy a weight, causing the head of the victim to be dashed against the crossbar. One observer noted more than a few balanced faces among the spectators as the prisoner's head was crushed before their eyes. Strong stomachs were necessary for both the spectators and executioners." (Gila County Historical Society.)

Jerry Ryan's brother, Lawrence, and sister, Kate, also came to Globe. Kate arrived from St. Louis, Missouri, in February 1886. She married Hugh Conahan, a native of Scotland, in December of that year. Lawrence moved to Globe in June 1889, as he found the climate more beneficial for his health than St. Louis. (JRB.)

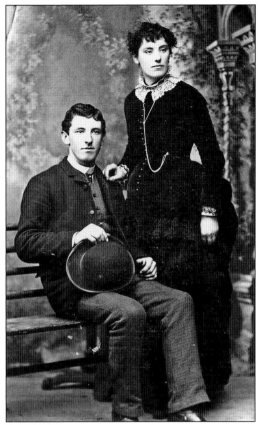

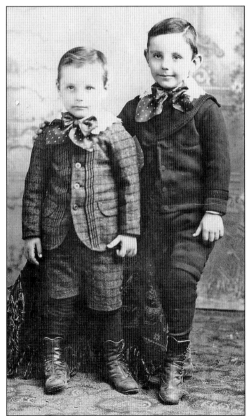

Jerry and Hugh Conahan, sons of Hugh and Kate (Ryan) Conahan, pose for photographer A. Miller in Globe. In September 1888, the *Silver Belt* announced Andrew Miller was in Globe to remain a short time only. Photographers who traveled the territory created an invaluable photographic record of Arizona's early days. (JRB.)

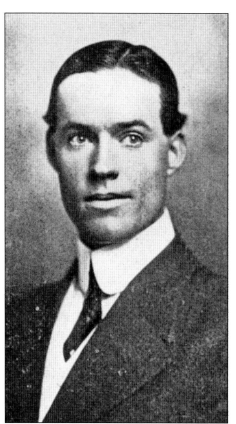

J. J. Kelly was born in Tombstone in 1887, the son of Irish parents Michael and Julia (Sullivan) Kelly. A well-known politician in Greenlee County, J. J. served a term as U.S. commissioner. He was promoted to assistant cashier of the First National Bank of Clifton in 1913. (*Who's Who in Arizona*, 1913.)

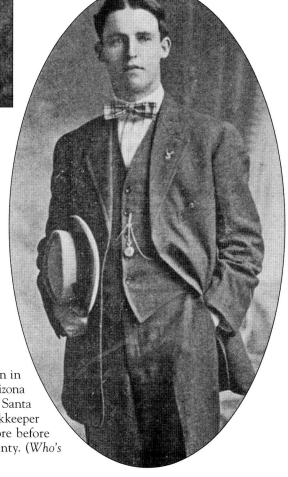

William E. Kelly, brother of J. J., was born in Tombstone in 1889. He was educated in Arizona public schools and St. Michael's College in Santa Fe, New Mexico. William was chief bookkeeper for the Shannon Copper Company store before being elected recorder of Greenlee County. (*Who's Who in Arizona*, 1913.)

James Dunseath was born in Belfast, Ireland, in 1873. At the age of 14, his family moved to Canada. After obtaining a law degree, Dunseath took a business trip to Morenci in 1902 that revealed the opportunities awaiting in Arizona. Dunseath was admitted to the bar with a specialty in land and mining law. In 1912, he was appointed U.S. commissioner of Tucson. (*Who's Who in Arizona*, 1913.)

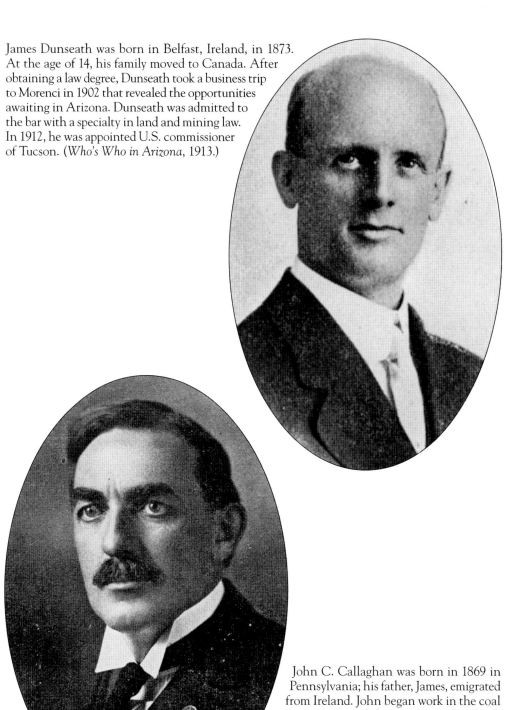

John C. Callaghan was born in 1869 in Pennsylvania; his father, James, emigrated from Ireland. John began work in the coal mines at age 11 while attending night school. Callaghan arrived in Arizona in 1898 and worked in the office of the Arizona Copper Company in Clifton, then the Copper Queen store in Bisbee. He was elected as Arizona state auditor in 1911 and served on many state boards and commissions. (*Who's Who in Arizona*, 1913.)

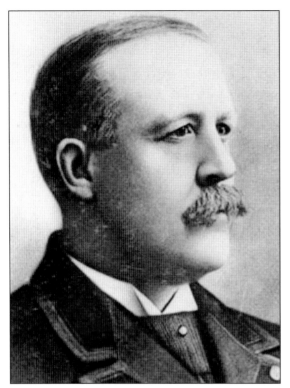

Nathan Oakes Murphy, descendant of early Irish immigrants to Maine, was the only governor of the Arizona Territory appointed on two non-consecutive occasions. He also represented Arizona in the United States House of Representatives. His administration organized the Arizona Rangers and established the Normal School (now Northern Arizona University) in Flagstaff. "Oakes," as he was called, was also involved in mining and railroads, his brother Frank M. being an early Arizona entrepreneur. (Arizona State Library, Archives and Public Records, History and Archives Division, Phoenix #96.1389.)

Sam Black and his brothers Matt, James, and George came to Flagstaff in the late 1800s. They were descendants of the Levels, who emigrated from County Galway to the Irish Corner District of West Virginia in the early 1800s. Sam served as city marshal for Flagstaff and was an Arizona Ranger. (B. W. Bryson.)

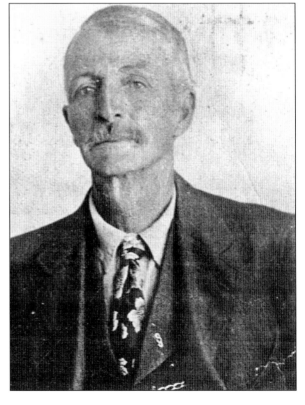

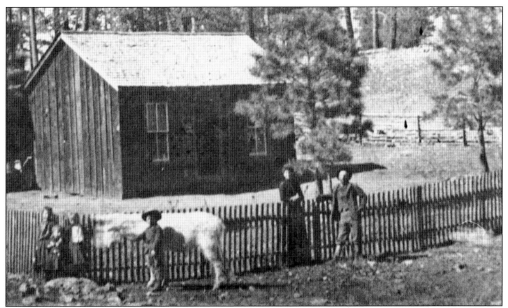

The Black family, from left to right, are daughters Creola, Bertha, and Lulu; son, Bernard; wife, Mary Jane; and husband, Sam. They are pictured at their ranch near Flagstaff. (B. W. Bryson.)

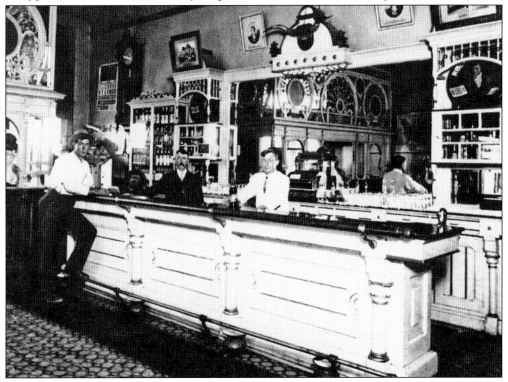

The Blacks, in addition to being in the cattle business, ran the livery, sales, and exchange stables. Sam's son, Bernard "Bum" Black, is shown on the right at Black's Bar with unidentified men. Bum was regarded for his skill as a wrangler, served as a deputy sheriff, and once headed off a fight between 30 Mexicans and cowboys in front of the saloon. (B. W. Bryson.)

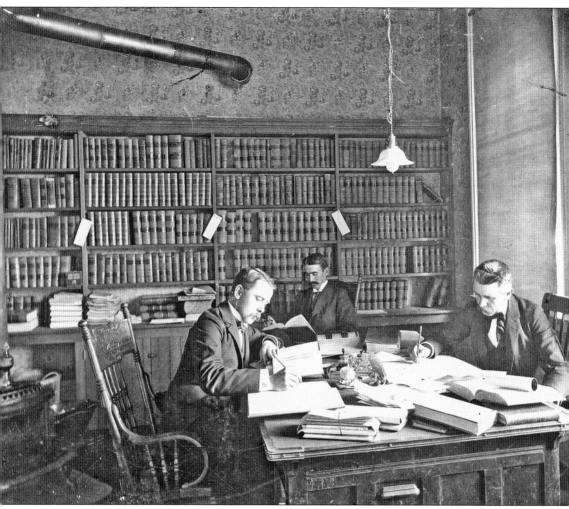

Joseph E. (left) and Robert Emmet Morrison (right) are pictured in their law firm in Prescott. The brothers were born in Chicago, their father having emigrated from County Antrim. In 1888, Robert practiced law in St. Johns and served as judge of Apache County. He moved to Yavapai County, serving as district attorney there. Robert was appointed U.S. attorney for the Arizona Territory in 1898 by President McKinley. His brother, Joseph, served as the assistant district attorney for Yavapai County before moving to Bisbee, where he did a great deal of business with Mexico. In 1912, President Taft appointed Joseph as U.S. attorney for the Arizona Territory. He held the unique position of being the last U.S. attorney for the Arizona Territory and the first for the newly-created State of Arizona. Joseph and Judge William Morrow organized the federal district court system for Arizona. The middle man is unidentified. (Sharlot Hall Museum.)

William James "Billy" Murphy was born in New York in 1854, the son of Irish parents. He traveled to the Globe area, meeting Julia O'Connell in McMillan, and the two eloped to Globe. Murphy served as sheriff of Pinal County. When Gila County was created in 1881, he was appointed sheriff by Gov. John C. Fremont. After a few months as sheriff, Murphy began working on many of the leading mines in the territory. In 1898, Murphy was working as superintendent of the Trilby Mine near Hot Springs Junction. A shoot-out with two men over trespassing ended his life. (William and Bonnie Murphy.)

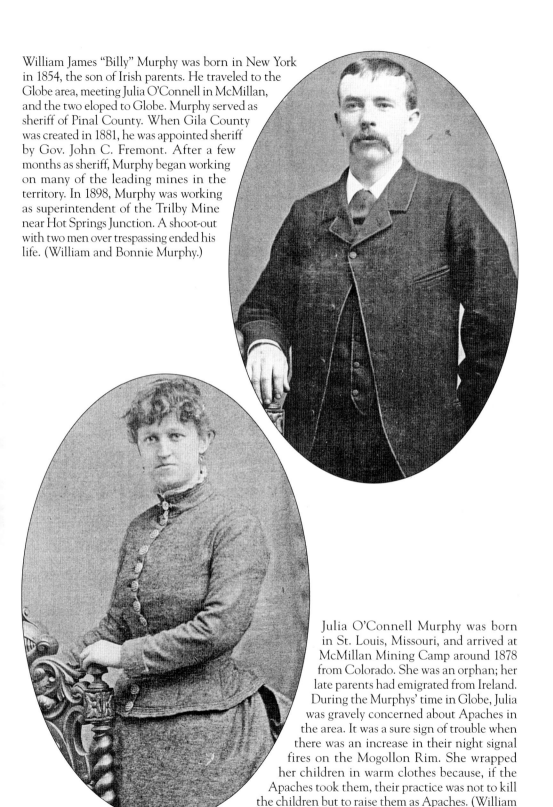

Julia O'Connell Murphy was born in St. Louis, Missouri, and arrived at McMillan Mining Camp around 1878 from Colorado. She was an orphan; her late parents had emigrated from Ireland. During the Murphys' time in Globe, Julia was gravely concerned about Apaches in the area. It was a sure sign of trouble when there was an increase in their night signal fires on the Mogollon Rim. She wrapped her children in warm clothes because, if the Apaches took them, their practice was not to kill the children but to raise them as Apaches. (William and Bonnie Murphy.)

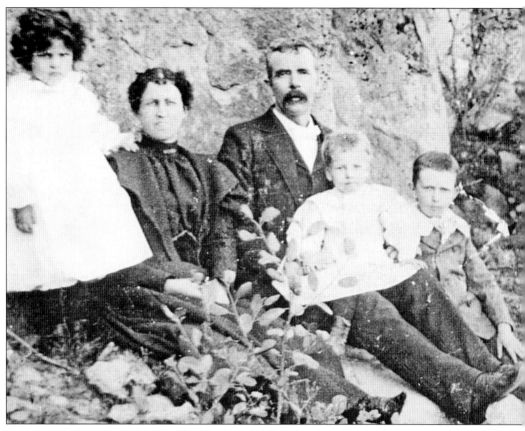

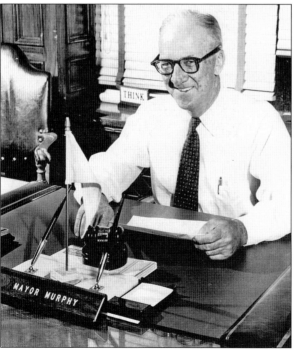

Frank Murphy, son of William and Julia, was elected on the reform ticket to the Phoenix City Council, of which Barry Goldwater was also a member. He served two terms as councilman and as mayor of Phoenix from 1956 to 1958. Frank was elected as state senator from Maricopa County and served two terms on the Arizona Industrial Commission, appointed by two governors. (William and Bonnie Murphy.)

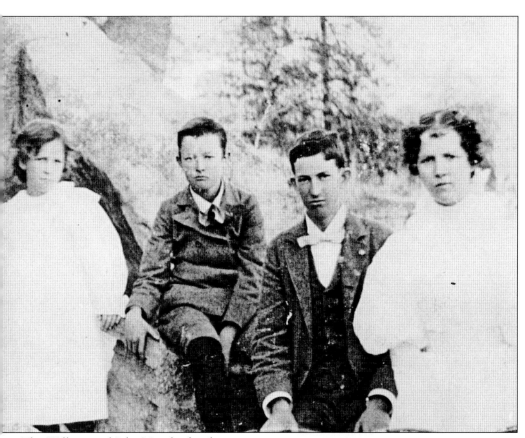

The William and Julia Murphy family are pictured enjoying a picnic at Granite Dells near Prescott in 1889. From left to right are Anna, Julia, William, Frank, Harry, Sue, Jack, Will, and Percy. The couple's youngest child, Walter, was born five months after his father's death. (William and Bonnie Murphy.)

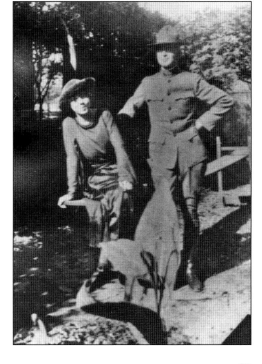

Wisconsin native M. J. Dougherty was descended from County Cork immigrants. After college graduation and teaching, he came to Mesa, establishing himself as a lawyer. In 1909, Dougherty married college classmate Bess Severn. He was a veteran of World War I, leaving the armed services as a lieutenant colonel. From 1920 to 1934, he served as state aide to the secretary of war. (Dougherty Foundation.)

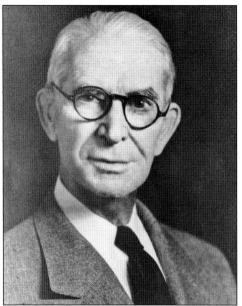

M. J. Dougherty served as Mesa's city attorney for 24 years. He authored the first Irrigation District Law, Interstate Stream Commission Act, and Arizona Power Authority Act. He was a partner in the law firm of Dougherty and Conner. Although M. J. and his wife, Bess, were childless, they had a keen interest in higher education, establishing the Dougherty Foundation to help deserving students reach their education goals through scholarships and student loans. (Dougherty Foundation.)

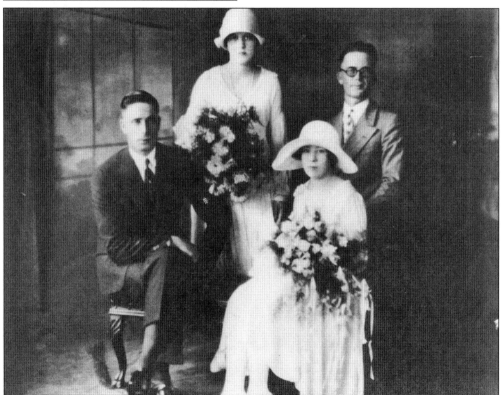

Active in agriculture and the cattle business, M. J. Dougherty joined with five other farmers and operated the first cotton gin in Arizona. Finding success here, M. J. encouraged his brothers to settle in Arizona. M. J.'s brother William (seated left) is pictured with his wife, Marguerite, standing behind him on their wedding day. Brother Joseph is standing behind his wife, Pearl. (Forrest Dougherty.)

A native of County Mayo, Ireland, William P. "Bill" Mahoney Sr. came to America at 18. Between 1900 and 1912, he worked in mines at Chloride and White Hills. In 1912, he organized Arizona's first miner's union, the Snowball Miners at Oatman in Mohave County. He was elected to the Arizona House of Representatives in 1914 and the following year married Alice Fitzgerald of Prescott. Elected to the state senate in 1916, his legislative career included cosponsoring measures dealing with minimum wages for women and workmen's compensation. Mahoney was sheriff of Mohave County from 1918 to 1926. In 1936, Gov. R. C. Stanford appointed him to the first State Board of Public Welfare. (Gladys Mahoney.)

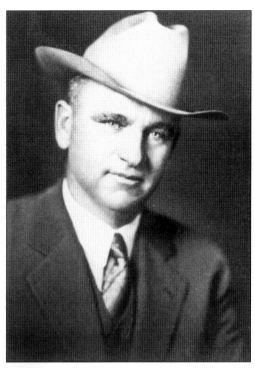

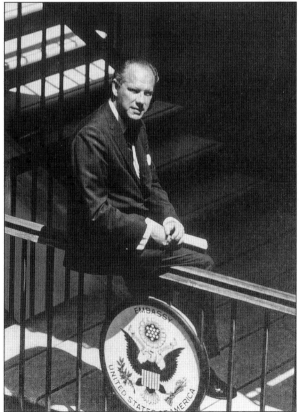

William P. "Bill" Mahoney Jr. won a scholarship to the University of Notre Dame, where he earned a law degree. He married Alice Doyle of San Francisco in 1946 and helped found the Phoenix Council of Civic Unity in 1947 to fight segregation. Thanks to his efforts, Phoenix schools desegregated in 1953. Mahoney was twice elected Maricopa County attorney. Due to his involvement with John Kennedy's presidential campaign and his civil rights record, Mahoney was appointed ambassador to Ghana in 1962. He worked tirelessly to improve conditions for the Navajo Nation as the founding member of the Navajo legal aid group, Dinebeiina Nahiilna Be Agaditahe. (Gladys Mahoney.)

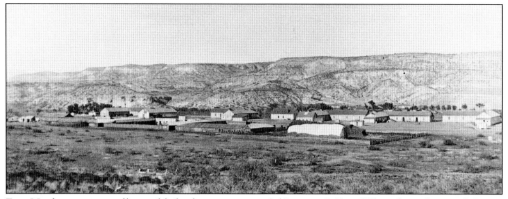

Fort Verde was originally established as an outpost of Prescott's Fort Whipple and named Camp Lincoln in honor of President Lincoln. Regular troops arrived in 1866, and the name was changed to Camp Verde, then Fort Verde. That year, Galway native Pvt. John Broderick was warned against going out fishing alone on the Verde River. Attacked by Native Americans, his body was found pierced by eight arrows and his scalp taken. (Arizona Historical Society/Tucson #49603.)

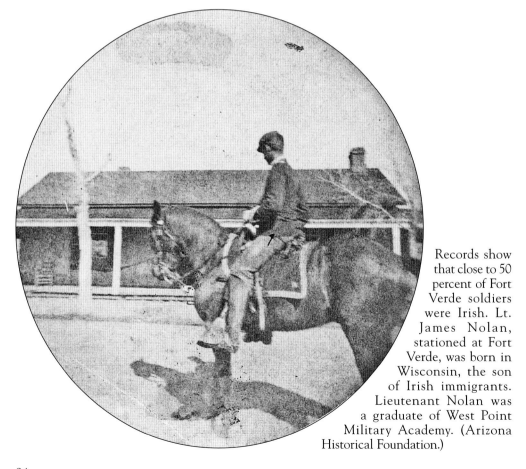

Records show that close to 50 percent of Fort Verde soldiers were Irish. Lt. James Nolan, stationed at Fort Verde, was born in Wisconsin, the son of Irish immigrants. Lieutenant Nolan was a graduate of West Point Military Academy. (Arizona Historical Foundation.)

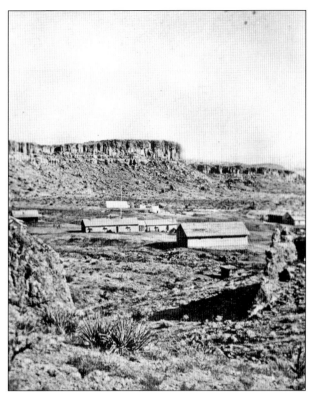

Lt. Edward Fitzgerald Beale, U.S. Navy, found two springs in Mohave County during an 1857 visit. Reports of skirmishes state Native Americans were attacking a mail station at Beale Springs and shooting all the stock belonging to the mail company. In 1871, Camp Beale was established under the command of Capt. Thomas Byrne of the 12th Infantry. *Arizona Place Names* notes that the redheaded Irishman handled the Native Americans with consummate skill. He had a small contingent of men but had a "deludherin' tongue" with which he beguiled the Native Americans in the cause of peace. (Photograph by D. P. Flanders; Mohave County Historical Society #1554.)

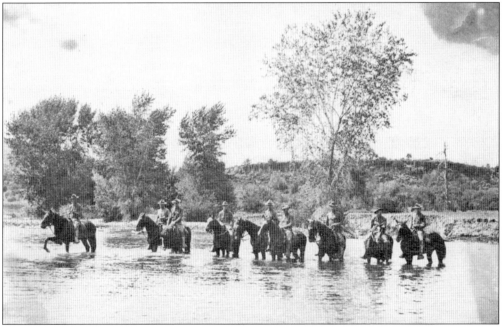

Fort Apache was established in 1870 on the east fork of White River. The 1880 census records show 222 individuals at the fort. Military men included two sons of Irish parents and 39 native-born Irish. This picture of cavalrymen from Fort Apache was taken around 1915 on the Apache Reservation. (JRB.)

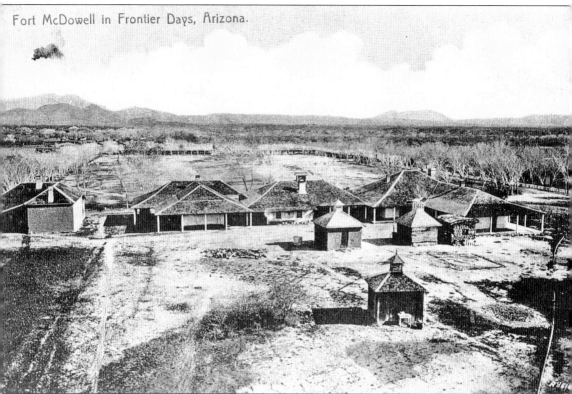

Fort McDowell in Frontier Days, Arizona.

Annie Dowling emigrated from County Kerry with her family around 1846 during the famine years. She married Patrick White, also from County Kerry, in 1858. Following Patrick's service in the Civil War, the Whites were sent to Wyoming, then on to Fort McDowell, Arizona. Patrick was discharged in 1876 after 20 years of service. He bought land near the fort to raise produce and livestock to sell to the post trader, adding to his land when the homestead laws allowed discharged soldiers to claim 640 acres. Capt. Adna Chaffee became commander of Fort McDowell, and word spread that he and Lt. Henry Kearney wanted the Whites off their property, claiming part was on the military reservation. In 1880, soldiers from the fort burned the Whites' home and used the cattle for target practice; Patrick was lost three days in the desert. The Whites moved to Tempe, where Patrick died in 1885. Annie continued her fight for justice in the burning of her property until 1905, when she was awarded $45,000 in damages and an apology from the U.S. Army. (Arizona Historical Foundation.)

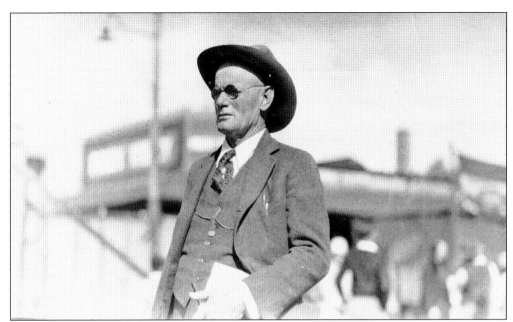

Ned White was born in Cheyenne, Wyoming, in 1873 to Irish immigrant parents Patrick and Annie White. Like his brothers, he worked in law enforcement in Cochise County, Arizona. He became a poet, "The Bard of Brewery Gulch." He lived in Arizona and wrote about its characters and attributes for the rest of his life. He wrote "The Day of the Sagebrush is Gone" in honor of Arizona's 1912 Admission Day. (Arizona Historical Society/Tucson #1101.)

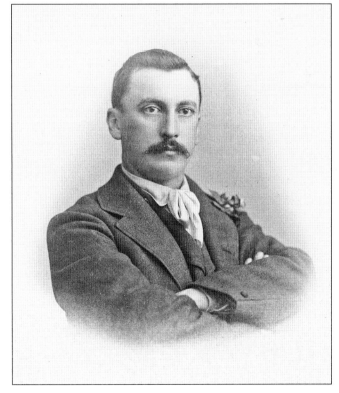

William Owen "Buckey" O'Neill appears to have been everywhere in the Arizona Territory. He was born in St. Louis, the son of an Irish father who fought in Meagher's Civil War regiment. O'Neill was a newspaper reporter and editor. He served as a captain in the Prescott Grays and as a special deputy in Phoenix, probate judge and sheriff of Yavapai County, and mayor of Prescott. His wife, Pauline Schindler, was active in women's suffrage. (Arizona Historical Foundation.)

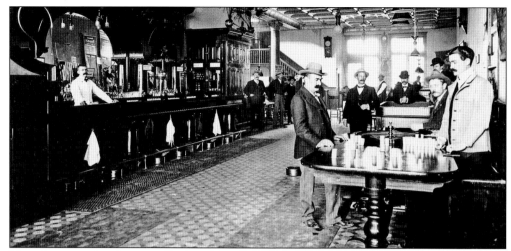

Upon his arrival in Prescott, Buckey O'Neill frequented the saloons along Whiskey Row. His favorite game of chance was faro. The game is illegal today, as odds favor the house by a factor of 67 percent. "Bucking the Tiger" became vernacular for the game to call the turning of three cards. Playing faro earned Buckey his nickname. Unidentified patrons are trying their luck in a Prescott saloon. (Arizona Historical Foundation.)

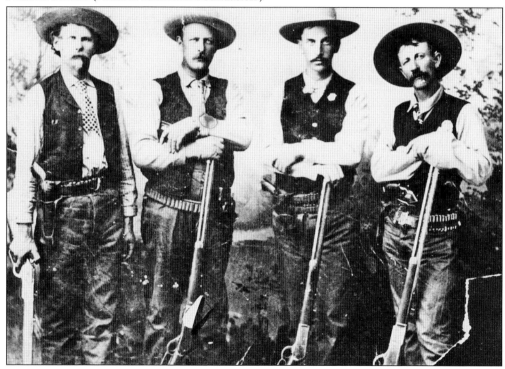

Buckey O'Neill, second from right, and his posse (from left to right), Carl Holton, Ed St. Clair, and Jim Black, are pictured at the time of the Canyon Diablo train robbery in March 1889. The A&P passenger train was robbed at gunpoint of $7,000 in cash and miscellaneous jewelry. The posse followed four outlaws into southern Utah and arrested them after three weeks, covering a trail of 600 miles. Jim Black was also Irish, his family having immigrated to America in the early 1800s. (B. W. Bryson.)

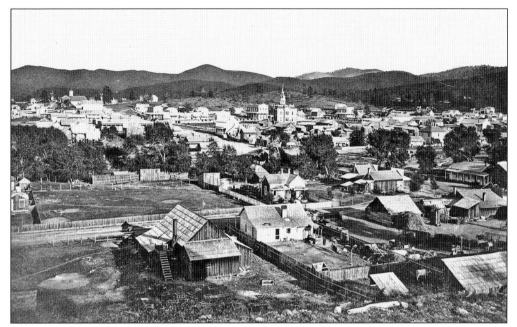

This bird's-eye view of Prescott is taken from Gurley Street. The county courthouse tower can be seen in the middle of the picture. In March 1889, Buckey O'Neill persuaded the Board of Supervisors of Yavapai County to buy 100 box elder trees that were planted around the courthouse plaza by the prisoners. (Arizona Historical Foundation.)

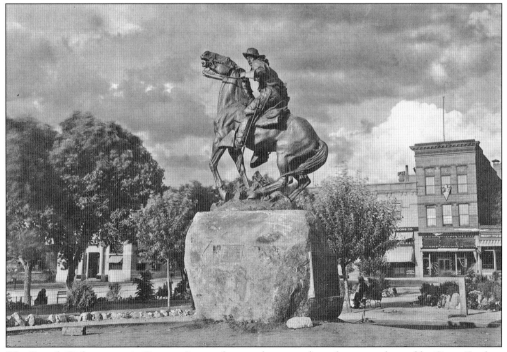

The Rough Rider statue in Prescott's courthouse plaza stands under trees planted by Capt. Buckey O'Neill. A member of Teddy Roosevelt's Rough Riders, O'Neill was killed on San Juan Hill in Cuba in 1898. (Arizona Historical Foundation.)

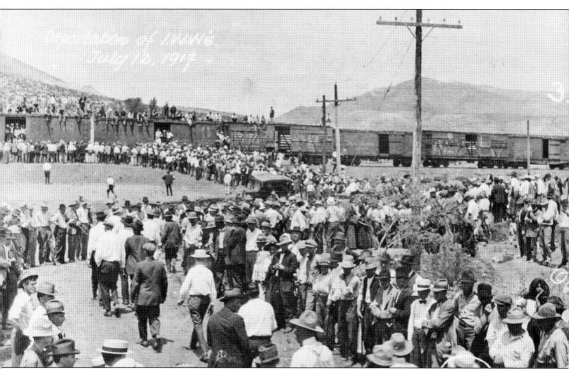

Unions, big business, economics, and ethnic bias provoked the Bisbee Deportation of 1917. European immigrants were many of the 5,000 miners who kept Bisbee humming. Before 1917, union activity was minimal, but the Industrial Workers of the World (IWW) began to gain strength. On June 24, 1917, the IWW submitted demands to Bisbee mining companies, including improved safety conditions and equal treatment for minority and foreign-born miners. The demands were rejected; half of the Bisbee workforce went out on strike. On July 12, 1917, 2,000 vigilante "deputies" began rounding up strikers. Those who refused to surrender were loaded into filthy boxcars, taken by train, and dumped in Hermanas, New Mexico. A train carrying food and water arrived later, but the men were without shelter for two days until American troops picked them up. Pres. Woodrow Wilson set up a commission to investigate the Bisbee deportation, resulting in groundbreaking legal precedents. The commission ruled the mining companies, not the IWW, were at fault in the deportation. Of the 1,186 deportees, the 67 Irish were the third-largest non-American population represented. (Arizona Historical Society/Tucson #44116.)

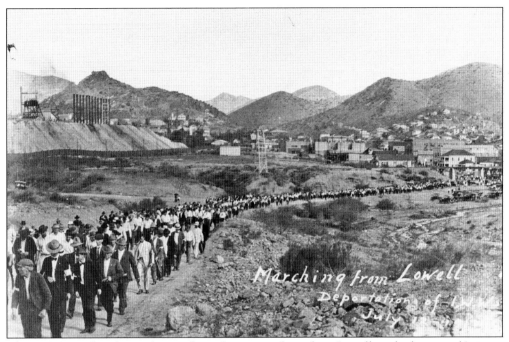

The IWW members being deported are shown marching from Lowell to the boxcars. (Arizona Historical Society/Tucson #43174.)

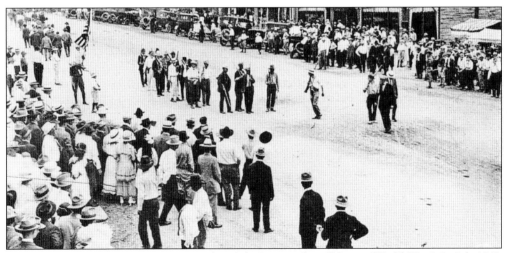

Tom Armer, son of Henry Armer, served as Gila County sheriff during World War I. In July 1917, it appeared that strikers from the Old Dominion Mine would create trouble. Armer organized the home guard, with each adult male being deputized and provided with a rifle. Members of the guard are shown drilling in front of a crowd of onlookers. The 17th U.S. Cavalry arrived a few days later and helped control the situation. Armer was credited with preventing the same situation in the Globe-Miami area that resulted in the deportation at Bisbee. (Gila County Historical Society.)

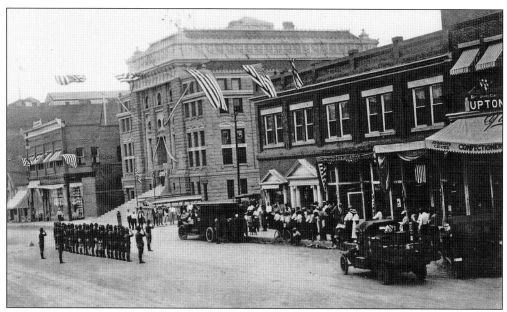

The Fourth of July Parade in Globe in 1918 included the 17th U.S. Cavalry after the army was called in for the Old Dominion strike. (JRB.)

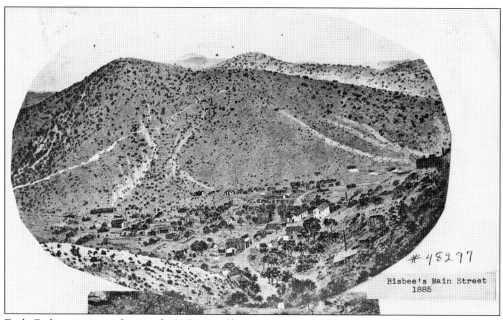

Early Bisbee is pictured around 1885. Not all men coming to Bisbee worked to better their lives. On December 8, 1883, five men held up the Goldwater Castaneda Store. The $7,000 Copper Queen Mine payroll was held for safekeeping there. The payroll had not arrived, and the angry men robbed the safe, staff, and customers. A shooting spree resulted, with four people being killed, including a pregnant woman. Saloon owner John Heath offered to help Sheriff Ward. The posse soon realized Heath was leading them on a false trail. (Arizona Historical Society/Tucson #48297.)

Arrested for the "Bisbee Massacre" were Dan Dowd, Red Sample, Tex Howard, and two Irishmen, Bill Delaney and Dan Kelly. John Heath was also arrested, convicted, and sentenced to life in Yuma prison. That verdict did not sit well with Cochise County citizens, and on February 22, 1884, a mob dragged Heath from his Tombstone cell and hanged him from a telegraph pole. The other five were tried and scheduled to be hanged March 8. Nellie Cashmen visited the condemned men in jail, as did Boxing champion John L. Sullivan, who was visiting Arizona. The men were buried in Tombstone's Boot Hill. (JRB.)

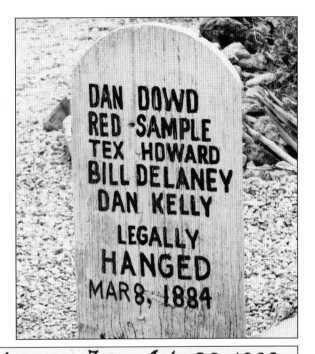

As was the custom of the day, invitations were issued to witness hangings. Michael J. Brophy received an invitation to the hanging of William and Thomas Halderman. The brothers had shot and killed constable Frank Ainsworth and Teddy Moore in April 1899 when the lawmen came to arrest them for shooting cattle. (Stephen Brophy.)

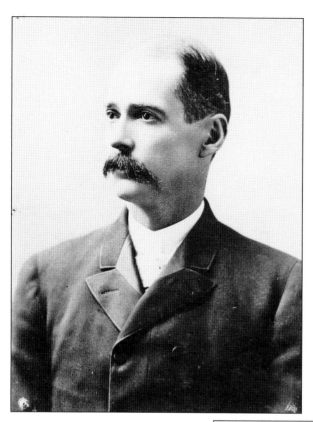

Johnny Behan was born in 1845 in Westport, Missouri, the son of Irish-born Peter Behan. He came to Arizona in the employ of the army and served as Yavapai County deputy and in various roles in the territorial legislature. He became part of Western legend when he failed to persuade the Earps and Clantons to lay down their guns and avoid the gunfight at the OK Corral. (Arizona State Library, History and Archives Division, Phoenix #97-6520.)

Jacob (Jack) Henry O'Neil Sr. was born about 1848, either in Pennsylvania or on a ship en route to the U.S. from Ireland. At age 13, Jack ran away twice to join the Union army, being made a drummer boy due to his young age. After his discharge in 1867, Jack settled in Fort Thomas, Arizona, where he was a known as a freighter, saloonkeeper, boardinghouse owner, and miner. In April 1881, he was appointed deputy sheriff for the Camp Thomas District by Graham County sheriff C. B. Rose. (Isabel Johns Perry.)

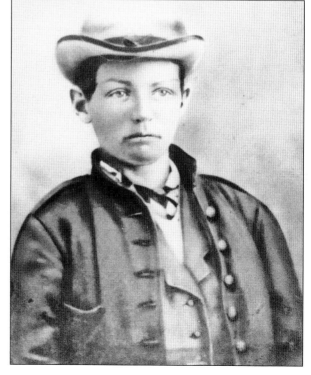

Four

RELIGION, EDUCATION, AND HEALING

Listen to the voices the next time you hear a news report from a disaster zone or the location of a large humanitarian activity somewhere around the world. Chances are you will hear at least one voice with an Irish accent.

This is not a new phenomenon. The Irish have never been shy about picking up and traveling to a new location, whether forced by extremity at home or lured by the promise of something better.

The deserts of Arizona could not be more of a contrast to the green hills of Ireland and the American cities that became a second home to many immigrants. Rough mining and farming communities that grew up from scratch needed every kind of service and expertise, from basic health care in the face of daily hazards to education once life was stable enough to allow families to prosper. And the Wild West's reputation for lawlessness and godlessness was a challenge for men and women of the cloth of every denomination.

If you walked down the street in an Arizona town 100 or more years ago, all you had to do was listen—you would have heard a stunning number of foreign accents, many of them Irish.

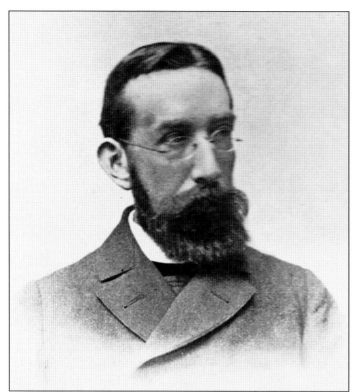

Fr. Eugene O'Growney was born August 25, 1863, at Ballyfallon, Athboy, County Meath, Ireland. O'Growney's family did not speak Irish (Gaelic); his passion for the language started when he was a young seminarian. He published a series of introductory Irish lessons in the *Weekly Freeman* that were first collected in 1894 as *Simple Lessons in Irish*. Learners like Lady Gregory and William Butler Yeats credited *Simple Lessons* as their resource for Irish language study, and tens of thousands of copies were distributed around the world. (*Leabhar an Athar Eoghan: The O'Growney Memorial Volume.*)

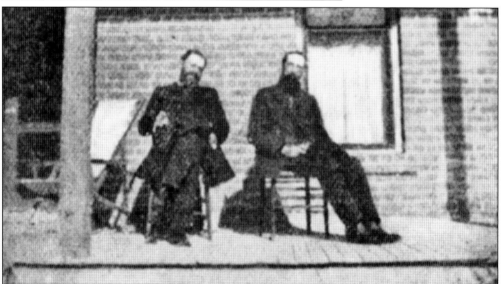

Due to tuberculosis, O'Growney relocated to San Francisco in November 1894. His condition did not improve, and he came to Arizona in early 1895 under the care of the Irish-born Sisters of Mercy; he was a patient at their sanatoriums in Phoenix, Yuma, and Prescott. O'Growney, right, enjoyed the company of locals, like Fr. F. Albert Quetu (left), who served in Prescott from 1889 to 1908. He continued writing for publications in the United States and Ireland, including an Irish-language translation of "The Star Spangled Banner." (*Leabhar an Athar Eoghan: The O'Growney Memorial Volume.*)

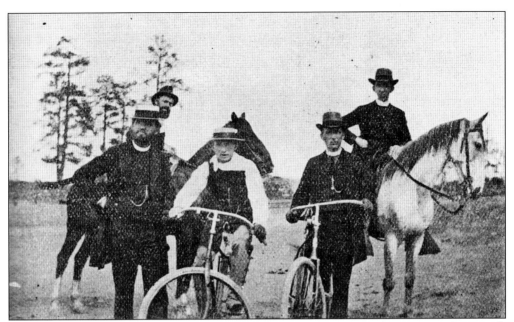

Father O'Growney visited Michael Riordan in Flagstaff and maintained a correspondence with him. As his health allowed, he enjoyed outdoor activities, although he never fully recovered. O'Growney is on the horse to the right; the other men are unidentified. O'Growney died in 1899 at Sisters Hospital in Los Angeles, California; he was buried at Calvary Cemetery. (*Leabhar an Athar Eoghan: The O'Growney Memorial Volume.*)

An t-Atair Eogan O'Gramna,
Mag-Nuadat.
Oide na Gaedilge.

By 1903, Gaelic Leaguers in Ireland and America raised enough money to exhume O'Growney's body, transporting it by train through San Francisco, Chicago, and New York, with memorial services along the way. His body now rests in a tomb on the grounds of St. Patrick's College, Maynooth, County Meath. Michael and Tim Riordan of Flagstaff contributed money to this effort. This calling card is in one of Michael Riordan's scrapbooks; in Irish, it states, "Father Eugene O'Growney, Maynooth, Irish (Gaelic) teacher." (Northern Arizona University, Cline Library, Riordan Family Collection.)

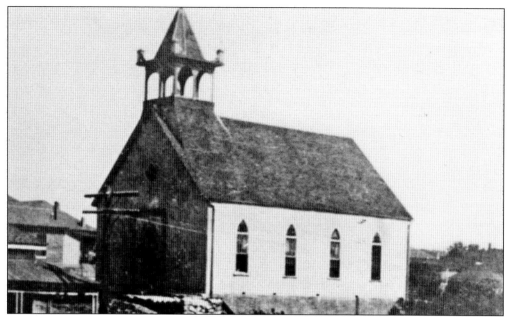

The Catholic priests in the early Arizona Territory rode a circuit through the mining camps and settlements. In August 1885, the *Silver Belt* noted that the ladies in Globe had taken the matter of erecting a Catholic church in charge. Committee members included Mrs. Kennedy, Mrs. Walsh, Mrs. Ryan, Mrs. Shanley, Mrs. Thompson, Mrs. Krentz, and Mrs. Atkins. The final fund-raiser was a St. Patrick's Day ball held in 1890. The proceeds from the ball completed the funds necessary to purchase the Baptist church. The newspaper noted that although the church was not as large as St. Peter's in Rome, it was amply sufficient. (Gila County Historical Society.)

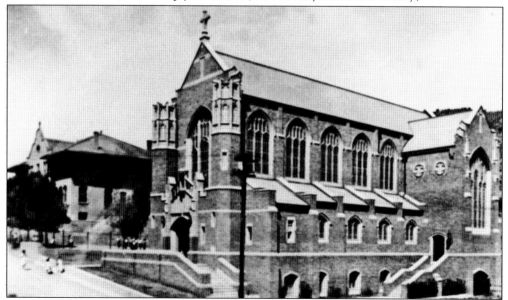

St. Patrick's Roman Catholic Church in Bisbee was built in 1916. It is a basilican structure in the Gothic Revival style with 31 Victorian stained-glass windows designed by Emil Frei Studios in St. Louis. The church was modeled after St. Begh's in Winterhaven, England. (Bisbee Mining and Historical Museum.)

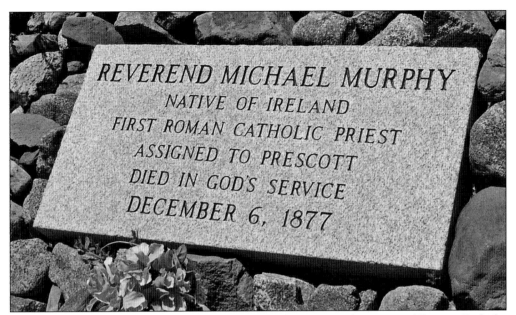

Fr. Michael Murphy, an Irish-born priest, came to Prescott as its first assigned Roman Catholic priest in October 1877. He had tuberculosis when he arrived, and his condition allowed him to celebrate mass at Luke's Hall only twice. He died on December 6, 1877, in the post hospital at Fort Whipple and was buried in Citizens Cemetery in Prescott. Irish priests came to Arizona as a mission territory into the 20th century. (KSW.)

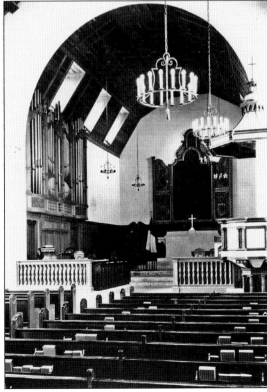

The perception that all Irish immigrants were Catholic was incorrect. Many individuals arriving in Arizona, particularly from Northern Ireland, were protestant. A number of them attended the Episcopal Church, the American equivalent of the Church of England and the Church of Ireland. The Episcopal Cathedral in Phoenix is pictured here. (Phoenix Public Library, Arizona Room, McClintock Collection.)

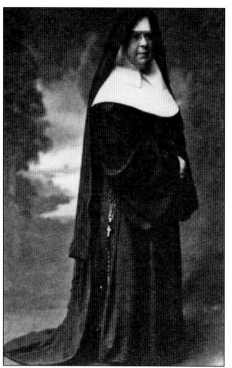

The skills and drive of Catholic pioneers found fertile ground in the American Southwest. The Sisters of Mercy were founded in Dublin, Ireland, in 1835 by Mother Mary Catherine McAuley, and requests for their services soon came from the United States. In 1880, Mother Mary Josephine Brennan brought a group of Sisters to Mesilla, New Mexico; by 1890, Mother Mary Paul O'Grady, pictured here, had sent sisters to Arizona to set up schools. (Sisters of Mercy, Burlingame Community.)

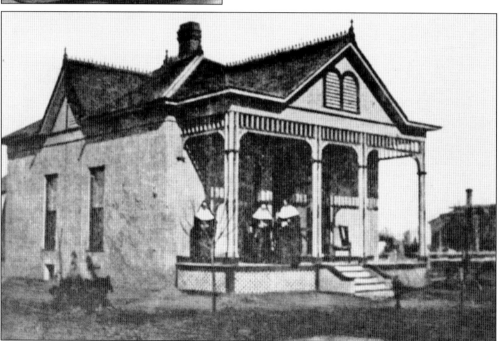

The Sisters of Mercy set up a school in Phoenix in 1892, but they found their calling among tuberculosis sufferers who came to the desert seeking health. In 1895, they rented a six-room brick house and opened St. Joseph's Sanatorium. They had to be financially creative; Sr. Mary Peter McTernan sought donations from people all over the territory, like Daniel W. O'Carroll, an Irish-born miner living in Winkelman. (Sisters of Mercy, Burlingame Community.)

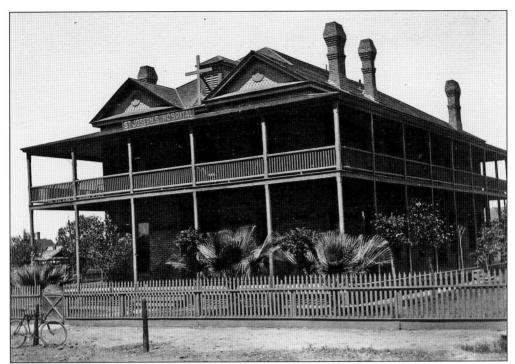

On March 19, 1895, a stake was driven into the ground at Fourth and Polk Streets in Phoenix to mark the location of St. Joseph's Hospital, which opened in the fall. The hospital—and the sisters—endured expansions, a 1917 fire, and the 1918 influenza epidemic. (Arizona Historical Foundation, McClintock Collection.)

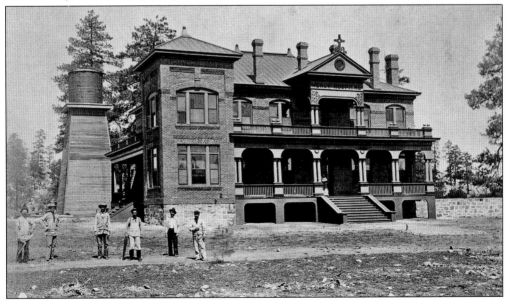

The sisters opened Mercy Hospital in Prescott on March 19, 1897. A benefactor was Dr. J. B. McNally, a native-born Irishman and division chief surgeon of the Santa Fe Railroad. Frank M. Murphy, president of the Santa Fe in Arizona, obtained the railroad contract for the sisters, who have operated hospitals all over the state. (Arizona Historical Foundation.)

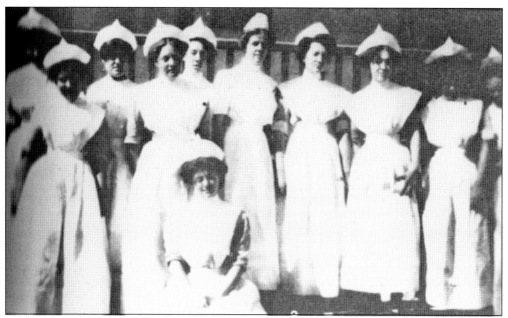

In 1910, Grace O'Brien and Anne Sullivan opened the School of Nursing at St. Joseph's Hospital in Phoenix, Arizona, the state's first nursing school. The nursing students shown here are unidentified. (Sisters of Mercy, Burlingame Community.)

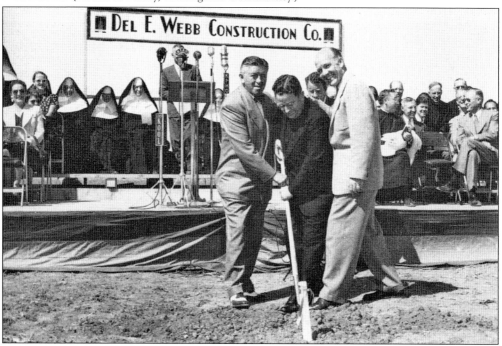

Ground was broken on April 3, 1951, on the site of a dairy farm at Third Avenue and Thomas Road in Phoenix for a new St. Joseph's Hospital. Despite early criticism for locating out in the country too far from town, the hospital has grown over the years, with many firsts to its credit. Wielding the shovel are, from left to right, Robert Becker of Del E. Webb Construction Company, Msgr. Robert Donohoe, and Gov. Howard Pyle. (Sisters of Mercy, Burlingame Community.)

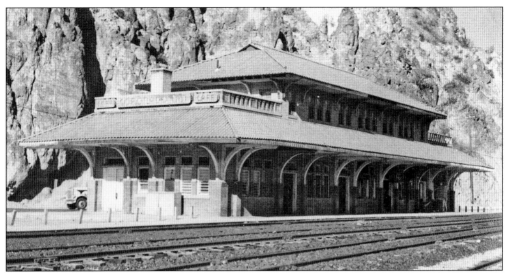

In the mid-19th century, aid societies in eastern cities organized "orphan trains" to transport homeless children to the rural Midwest, believing they would benefit from growing up in such an environment. Many of these orphans were Irish Catholics, viewed through the rampant nativism of the time as racially and socially inferior. The Catholic Sisters of Charity sent 40 Irish Catholic children from their New York City foundling home to Arizona on an orphan train that arrived at the Clifton station in 1904. (Arizona State Library, History and Archives Division, Phoenix #84.4017.)

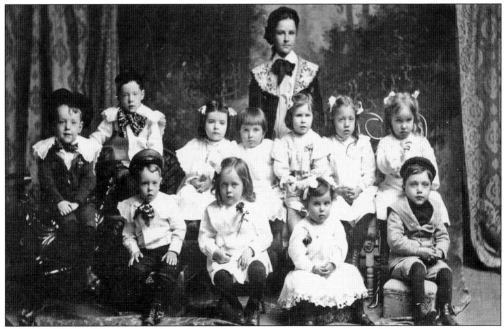

The local priest selected Mexican Catholic families to receive the children. Anglo vigilantes seized 19 of the children from the Mexican homes with the intention of adopting the children themselves. The Sisters of Charity sued to get the children back, but three courts, including the U.S. Supreme Court, upheld the vigilantes, who kept the children pictured here. (Phoenix Public Library, Arizona Room, McClintock Collection #211868849.)

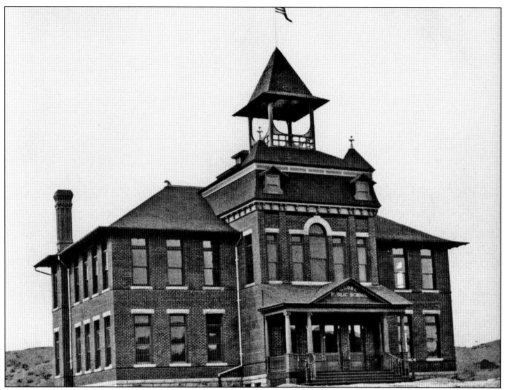

The Central School in Globe was built in 1897 at the cost of $7,000. A number of Irish names are listed among the students in 1901, including Ryan, Holohan, Donnelly, O'Neil, and Keegan. School records show that the eighth graders studied civics, physiology, first Latin, algebra, arithmetic, physical geography, English grammar, and bookkeeping. (Gila County Historical Society.)

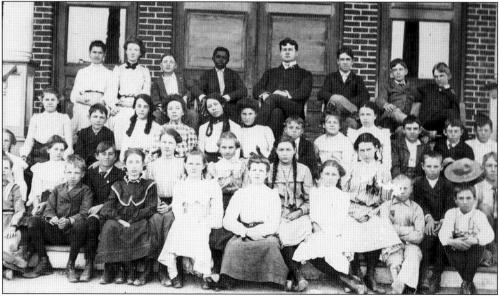

This photograph of the Central School students was taken around 1900. The only student identified is William Albert Ryan, holding his hat. (JRB.)

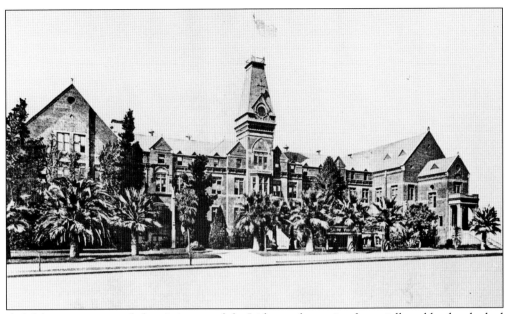

As life became more settled in Arizona and the Irish were becoming financially stable, they looked for higher education for their children, as none was available in the territory. St. Vincent's Catholic College in Los Angeles, founded in 1865, was the choice of a number of parents for their sons. Others chose St. Mary's College in Oakland, California, or St. Michael's in Santa Fe, New Mexico. (Loyola Marymount University Library, Department of Archives and Special Collections.)

Irish daughters were also provided with well-rounded educations. Eleanor "Nellie" Gleeson, the daughter of John and Elizabeth Gleeson, attended public schools in Arizona and New Mexico before completing her education at St. Mary's Academy in Los Angeles. She married Grover Pidgeon, chief engineer of the Copper Queen branch of the Phelps Dodge Corporation. (JRB.)

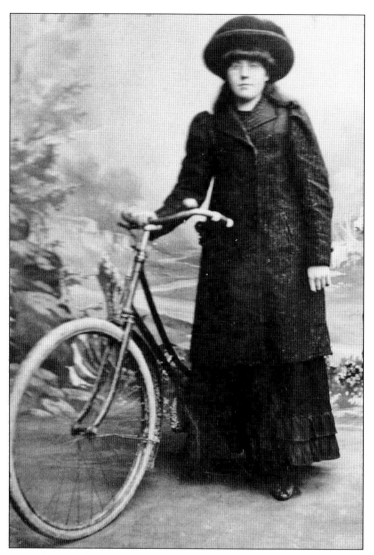

Josephine Murphy, the daughter of Denis and Margaret Murphy, is pictured in Ireland while attending school at Thurles. Returning to America to complete her education, she graduated from St. Mary's Academy in Los Angeles and a business college in San Diego. Her sister Marguerite also graduated from St. Mary's Academy. (JRB.)

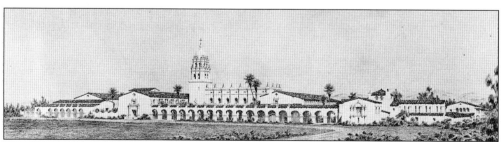

Ellen A. Brophy commissioned a series of stained-glass windows from Ireland for the student chapel at Brophy Preparatory School. The windows were designed and produced under the guidance of her friend Sarah Purser, who had set up An Túr Gloine, a pioneering cooperative stained-glass studio in Dublin. The studio embraced ideas of the Arts and Crafts movement and Irish nationalism. The windows were shipped from Ireland and installed in the chapel in the Arizona desert in 1933. (Arizona Historical Society/Tucson #MS1225H2792/H.)

Prof. A. J. Matthews, a New York native of Irish descent, was superintendent of Prescott schools before becoming president of Tempe Normal School, now Arizona State University. (*Who's Who in Arizona*, 1913.)

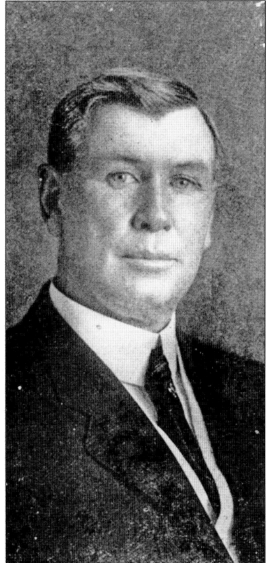

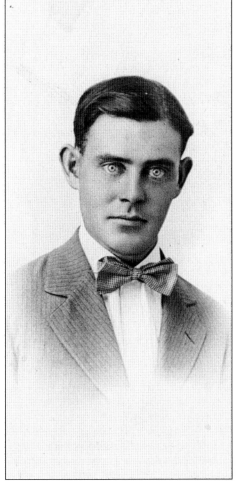

Edward Emmet Ryan's older brothers and sister were sent out of state to complete their education. With higher education progressing in Arizona, Edward Emmet and his younger sister, Alice, were able to attend school at what became the University of Arizona in Tucson. The land-grant college was established in October 1891. (JRB.)

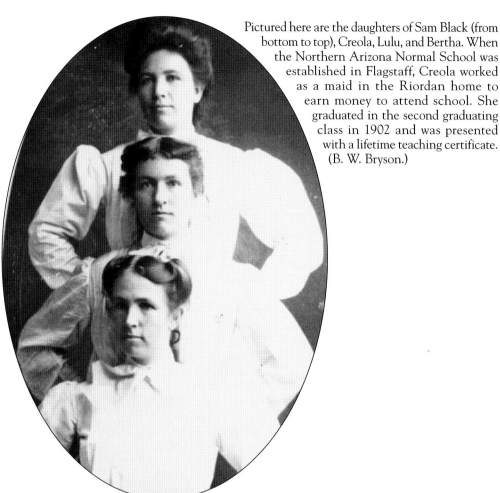

Pictured here are the daughters of Sam Black (from bottom to top), Creola, Lulu, and Bertha. When the Northern Arizona Normal School was established in Flagstaff, Creola worked as a maid in the Riordan home to earn money to attend school. She graduated in the second graduating class in 1902 and was presented with a lifetime teaching certificate. (B. W. Bryson.)

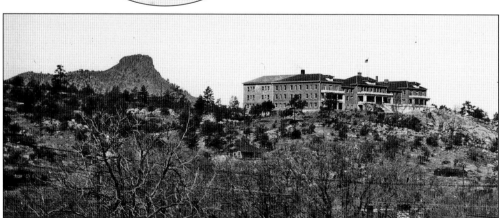

Three Prescott men, A. J. Doran, Frank M. Murphy, and Johnny Duke, had an idea in 1909 to create a retirement home for Arizona pioneers. Murphy donated land southwest of Prescott for construction of a brick building housing 40 men. In 1916, a women's wing was added to the facility. Still in operation, the facility houses 150 Arizona pioneers or disabled miners. Pioneers must have been residents of Arizona for 50 years. (Arizona Historical Foundation.)

Five

IRISH ARIZONA TODAY

Arizona's population increased after World War II, and the Irish culture in Arizona continued to grow. Tucson, as befits a city founded by Irishman Hugo O'Conor, has a very active Irish community. A St. Patrick's Day parade is held each March, as well as an annual Emerald Ball to celebrate the Irish. The city is home to the Tucson Celtic Festival and the Old Pueblo Feis. If you yearn for cooler climates, head to Flagstaff, home of the Northern Arizona Celtic Heritage Society and the Highland Celtic Festival, or to Prescott where the Prescott Area Celtic Society has been established. Arizona's Irish newspaper, the *Desert Shamrock*, is ably published by editor Julie O'Maher. The Arizona Irish Music Society keeps track of the Celtic music being played at the Irish pubs and various venues around Arizona. Five Irish dance schools are filled with students learning Irish dancing and competing in the feis competitions around Arizona and the United States. A number of accomplished Arizona students have competed at the world championships, held in Ireland.

The most visible Irish presence is the Irish Cultural Center, located at Hance Park in Phoenix. The center grew out of a cooperative public-private partnership between the City of Phoenix, the Arizona Department of Transportation, a sister city relationship with Ennis, Ireland, and the Irish Cultural and Learning Foundation, a local nonprofit coalition of affiliated Irish and Celtic organizations started by William O'Brien in 1998.

The center includes *An Halla Mór* (The Great Hall), built in the 1850s style of an Irish meeting hall; the replica of an 1800s County Clare farmhouse, the Irish Gift Shop, and a memorial to *An Gorta Mór*, the Great Hunger. A wrought iron pedestrian gate that opens to Central Avenue was donated by Jim and Judy Cunningham. The Howard Adams Gate and the Ken Clark Bench honor two men whose untiring efforts shaped the relationships and planning that made the Irish Cultural Center possible. At the time of publication, the Executive Committee for the Irish Cultural and Learning Foundation includes chairman of the board of trustees Jim Cunningham, Pres. Patricia Prior, Sec. Jim Daugherty, Treasurer Chuck Vallelonga, Vice Pres. John McMorrow, Chairman Emeritus Bill O'Brien, Consular Liaison Sean Lee, Architect Paul Ahern, and trustees Bill Quinn, Jimmy O'Connor, Denisa Casement, and Ed Cunningham.

The Academy of Irish and Celtic Studies is a major program of the center. The goal of the academy is to offer the highest-quality educational and cultural programming. The center's mission is to provide a link between the people of Arizona and the people of Ireland and other Celtic cultures.

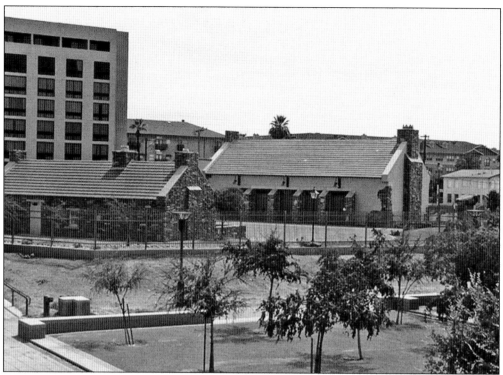
This view of the Irish Cultural Center in Phoenix was taken from the Central Avenue bridge crossing Hance Park. (desertshamrock.com.)

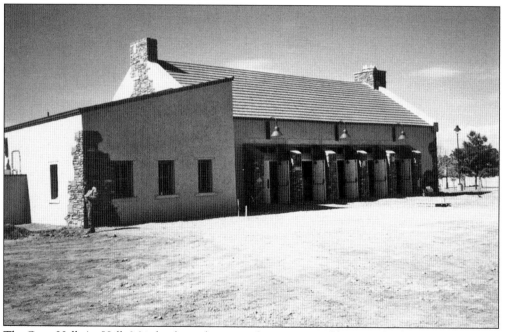
The Great Hall, An Halla Mór, has been the scene of many memorable events for the Irish community, including a visit from Irish president Mary Robinson. The Celtic Cultural Series has hosted Lunasa and Dervish from Ireland and Robin Huw Bowen from Wales. (desertshamrock.com.)

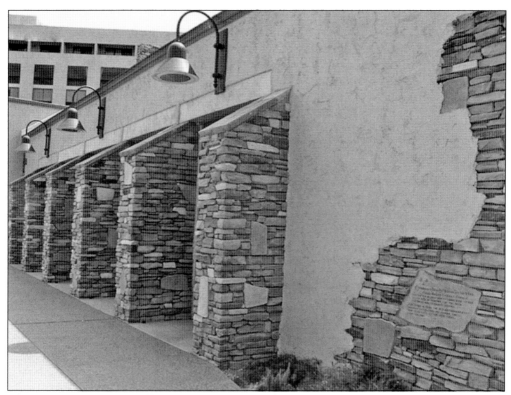

The cornerstone of An Halla Mór was a gift from Phoenix's sister city, Ennis, Ireland. The stone was from the historic Buttermarket Building in Ennis. (desertshamrock.com.)

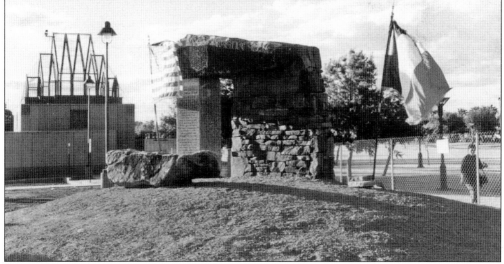

The An Gorta Mór (literally, "the great hunger" known as the Irish potato famine) Memorial honors the one-and-a-half million Irish who died of starvation and disease 150 years ago due to crop failure and social injustice. Between the years 1845 and 1850, more than one million Irish men and women immigrated to the United States. The arch reflects a Celtic passageway, symbolizing entry from the old world to the new. The inscription on the memorial is from a poem titled "The Famine" by Sean Prior. (desertshamrock.com.)

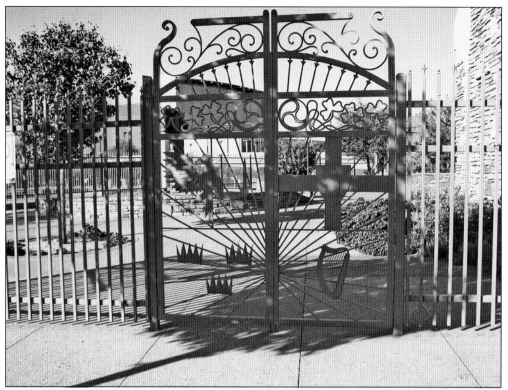

The Irish Foundation Gate features the symbols of the four provinces of Ireland: Ulster, Connaught, Leinster, and Munster. Founded in 1973, this organization was formed to bring together people of Irish heritage. The Irish Foundation sponsors Phoenix's Emerald Ball each year. (JRB.)

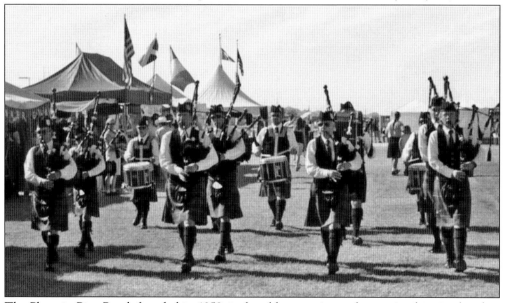

The Phoenix Pipe Band, founded in 1958, is the oldest continuously running bagpipe band in Arizona. Band members wear the red MacGregor tartan. Their repertoire includes traditional and modern Scottish and Irish music. (Phoenix Pipe Band.)

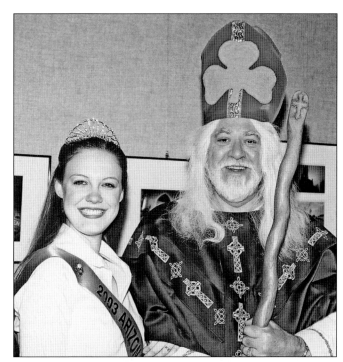

The 2003 Arizona Colleen, Erin Sweeney, is greeted by Saint Patrick (Don McMasters) himself. The Colleen Pageant is an event that encourages young girls to become a part of their Irish heritage, to share experiences with others of Irish descent, and to learn more about the Irish and their traditions. (desertshamrock.com.)

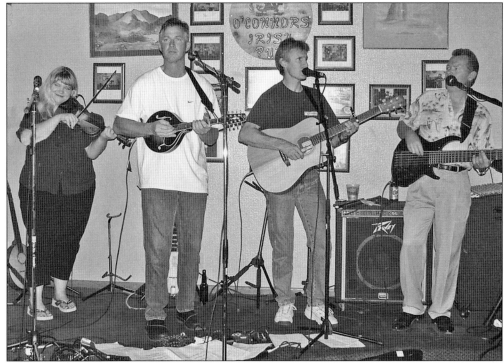

These Irish musicians are, from left to right, Jerica Leathers, Jerry McMorrow, John McMorrow, and Seamus King entertaining at O'Connor's Pub in Phoenix. Pub owner Jimmy O'Connor hails from Ballygar, County Galway, Ireland. After selling his software company, Jimmy decided it was a good time to fill "every Irishman's dream" and opened O'Connors. (desertshamrock.com.)

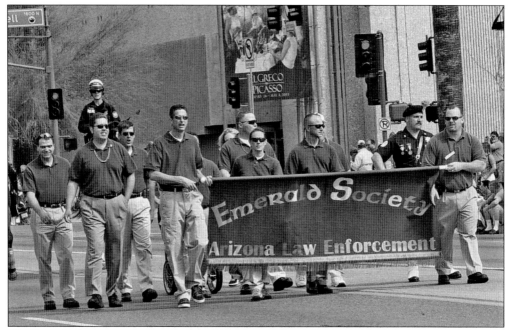

The Emerald Society is an organization of American police officers and firefighters of Irish heritage. Their goals include recognizing the accomplishments of Irish Americans in law enforcement and among firefighters as well as preserving the Irish culture. Arizona law enforcement members of the Emerald Society are shown marching in the 2003 St. Patrick's Day parade in Phoenix. (desertshamrock.com.)

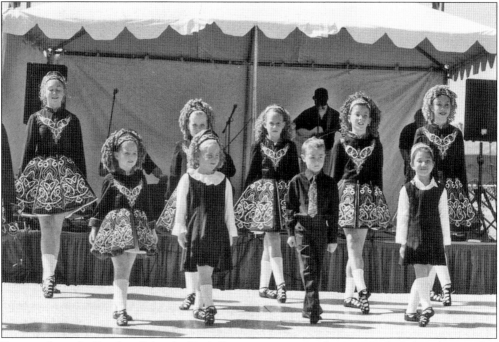

Dancers from the Bracken School of Irish Dance entertain at the 2003 Irish Cultural Festival at Hance Park. (desertshamrock.com.)

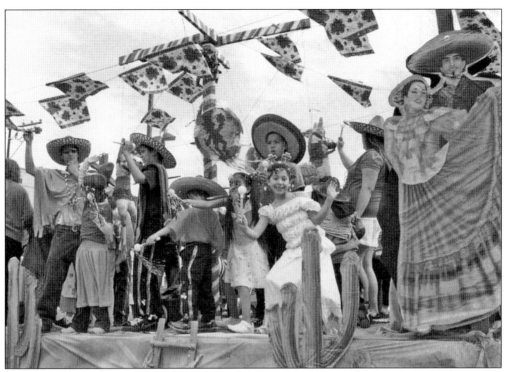

The McArdle Clan won Best Float in the 2008 Tucson St. Patrick's Day Parade. The parade theme was St. Patrick in the Old Pueblo. Roscommon, Ireland, is a sister city to Tucson. (Aine Ni Haralambie, www.tucsonirishcommunity.com.)

E. R. I. N. (Executive Resources for Irish Networking) sponsored a float in the 2003 Phoenix St. Patrick's Day Parade. E. R. I. N. is a business network for individuals with strong Irish heritage or interest. The Phoenix St. Patrick's Day Parade and Faire started in 1983 to enhance the heritage and traditions of Irish culture and share them with the rest of the state. (desertshamrock.com.)

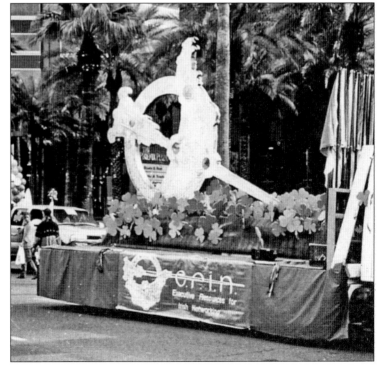

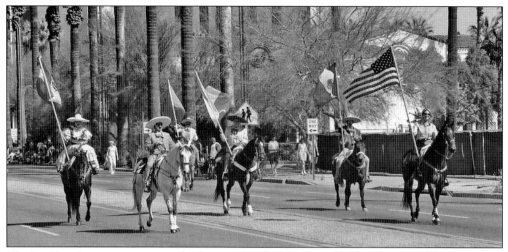

The Los San Patricios are pictured riding in the 2005 St. Patrick's Day Parade in Phoenix. Felix Corona, on the white horse, and William O'Brien, carrying the Irish flag, are the cofounders of the group honoring the bond of friendship born between the nations of Ireland and Mexico. In the 1850s, the St. Patrick's Battalion fought bravely for the cause of Mexico in the Mexican-American War, cementing a lasting friendship. (desertshamrock.com.)

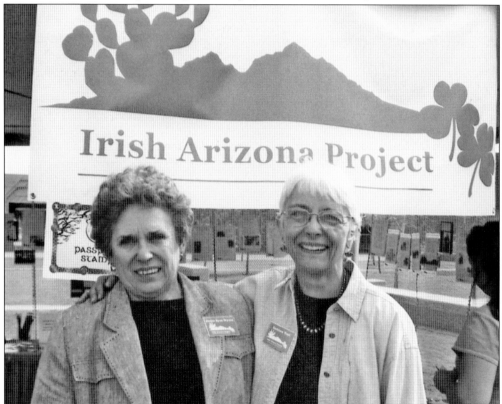

Coauthors Janice Ryan Bryson (left) and Kathy Shappee Wood (right) presented an exhibit of Irish Arizona history at the 2006 and 2007 Arizona Irish Festivals under the auspices of their nonprofit Irish Arizona Project. (JRB.)

BIBLIOGRAPHY

Anderson, Donna. *History of Globe Arizona*. Seattle: Classic Day Publishing, 2007.
Bailey, Lynn R. *We'll All Wear Silk Hats*. Tucson: Westernlore Press, 1994.
Ball, Larry D. *Desert Lawmen*. Albuquerque: University of New Mexico Press, 1992.
Barnes, Will C. *Arizona Place Names*. Tucson: University of Arizona Press, 1977.
Cline, Platt. *They Came to the Mountain*. Flagstaff: Northern Arizona University, 1976.
Frazier, Robert W. *Forts of the West*. Norman: University of Oklahoma Press, 1965.
Gordon, Linda. *The Great Arizona Orphan Abduction*. Cambridge, MA: Harvard University Press, 1999.
Mason, Robert. *The Burning*. Phoenix: Phoenix Publishing Group, 2000.
McKinney, Marion White. *Ned White: Arizona's Bard of Brewery Gulch*. Denver: Golden Bell Press, 1965.
O'Farrelly, Agnes. *Leabhar an Athar Eoghan: The O'Growney Memorial Volume*. Dublin, Ireland: M. H. Gill and Son, Ltd., 1904.
Radbourne, Allan. *Mickey Free*. Tucson: Arizona Historical Society, 2005.
Todd, Arthur Cecil. *The Cornish Miner in America*. Spokane, WA: Arthur H. Clark Company, 1995.
Walker, Dale L. *Death Was the Black Horse*. Austin, TX: Madrona Press, Inc., 1975.
Conners, Jo. *Who's Who in Arizona*. vol. 1. Tucson: Arizona Daily Star, 1913.

ACROSS AMERICA, PEOPLE ARE DISCOVERING
SOMETHING WONDERFUL. *THEIR HERITAGE.*

Arcadia Publishing is the leading local history publisher in the United States. With more than 4,000 titles in print and hundreds of new titles released every year, Arcadia has extensive specialized experience chronicling the history of communities and celebrating America's hidden stories, bringing to life the people, places, and events from the past. To discover the history of other communities across the nation, please visit:

www.arcadiapublishing.com

Customized search tools allow you to find regional history books about the town where you grew up, the cities where your friends and family live, the town where your parents met, or even that retirement spot you've been dreaming about.

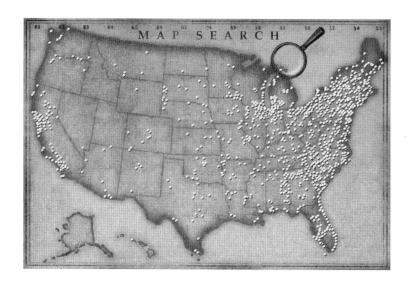